Career Awakening

—— *how to* ——

align your career with your Soul Purpose

Ruth Morgan

© Creating Healthy Careers 2022

Career Awakening

How to align your career with your Soul Purpose

Career Awakening
How to Align Your Career With Your Soul Purpose

Copyright 2022 Creating Healthy Careers
1st Edition, April 2022

All rights reserved. Other than for personal use, no part of this book may be reproduced in any way, in whole or part, without the written consent of the copyright holder.

PLEASE NOTE:
Career Awakening, How To Align Your Career With Your Soul Purpose is not intended to replace medical advice or treatment. The author of this book does not dispense medical advice. The intent of the author is only to offer information of a general nature to help you in your quest for spiritual wellbeing. If you are dealing with any sort of physical, mental or emotional disorders we suggest that you consult your physician or therapist and use the exercises and processes in this book under their supervision. Neither the author or publisher assumes any responsibility for your improper use of this book.

Published by IngramSpark
Cover design by Mersina
Layout by Creative Dzine (creativedzine99@gamil.com)
Edited by Catherine James Creative
ISBN: 978-0-6454458-0-0

© Creating Healthy Careers 2022

DEDICATION

I dedicate this book to my Mum, Dad and Grandad who were key influencers in showing me my path. And to my children, Alex and Zoe, who I'm so proud follow their own path in life.

Table of Contents

Introduction — 6

Chapter 1
AWAKEN: — 11
Recognising Wake-Up Calls

Chapter 2
EXPANSION: — 29
Learning What Life's Lessons Have Shown You About Your Soul Purpose

Chapter 3
CLEARING: — 45
Releasing What is Blocking Your Path

Chapter 4
CREATING: — 63
Clarity & Alignment

Chapter 5
EMERGENCE: — 92
Stepping Into the Person You Are Here To Become

Chapter 6
ATTRACTION: — 109
Create It, Feel It, Attract It

Chapter 7
SURRENDER: — 123
Trust & Gratitude

Introduction

I've heard many people say, "we all have a book inside us," and I'm sure they mean that we all have valuable lessons to share that we've learnt in life, once we've learnt them. Well I'm taking a different approach. When I started to write this book in the initial year of my business, I had no idea how it would end or if it would end! I wasn't sure what I would learn along the way, what the message or purpose was, and what I wanted to leave you with that would impact your career and life. I just knew I was on a crazy ride, and there had to be a purpose behind it, so I wanted to capture the story as it unfolded. So my approach to writing this book has been a bit like my life. I took a step I might not have been sure of, and the next step appeared in front of me. I didn't have it all worked out beforehand. We might think we've got a plan and are heading from A to B, but the Universe has different ideas in mind for us quite often, and with each step we take, the vision changes and becomes clearer.

When I started writing this book, my focus was on Creating Healthy Careers. Then, when I began observing patterns in mine and in my clients' lives, it became How to Create and Attract Your Dream Job. As I continued on the path and became bolder, I saw things from a bigger perspective, which led me to the message I want to convey with Career Awakening. You see, this book isn't for everyone. It's for those of you who have an inner knowing that there's something else for you in life, who want to contribute in a more meaningful way and for who having a career is more than just about earning an income. This book has spoken to you because you are on a path of self-discovery and fulfilling your life's purpose.

I started writing this book with the philosophy that action leads to inspiration, not the other way around. Quite often, people wait for inspiration to hit before they take action. However, I've found it's in taking action that something fabulous often emerges and inspiration kicks in. Now that I look back at how my business has evolved over the past four years, I could never have known what path it would take or what I would learn and create when I took those first baby steps into business. Some people may say it's a little crazy, putting everything on the line and not having a clear plan of how I was going to make it happen. I have learnt that if I try and figure it all out before I take action, I don't take any action – sound familiar? Looking back, I've realised that I was putting the principles of this book into practice before I even realised what they were!

What I know is that I've learnt many lessons when it comes to our careers, and I've observed enough people to notice familiar patterns occur time and time again. I know what people are looking for and what gets in their way. Plus, I've been in situations where I've tried a different approach to the typical way, and it worked. I want to share everything I know to help you succeed in your career so that it has a flow-on effect to your health, wealth and happiness, and to your family's. I wish you to avoid some of the mistakes I've made, but that would rob you of your life lessons that are all a part of helping you on your path. So here goes.

© Creating Healthy Careers 2022

My Why

Doing something you love isn't just a 'nice to have'. It's essential to your wellbeing, fulfilment, happiness and success, but more than that, it's a gateway to living your purpose.

It didn't start this way for me though. I grew up watching my Dad come home miserable from work, and just wanting him to be happy, you'll read a bit more about that in Chapters 1 & 2. Initially, my motivation for starting my business and this book was to help people be happy in their careers. I wanted to positively impact their health, home life, and their family's health because I have witnessed first-hand the formation of serious illness when someone lives with prolonged stress. My mother died at the age of 63 from breast cancer, having lived in a stressful household and with no history of breast cancer in her family. Now I'm not blaming Mum or Dad for the circumstances, and I can fully see both sides of the story and understand how stress manifests through our thoughts with hindsight. Unfortunately, this information wasn't common knowledge 40 or 50 years ago, and many people still live their lives without that awareness. I'm sharing this with the hope of waking people up to what can happen if you're not tuned into what's going on in your body, your mind, and your life, and not reading the signs to get back on your path. When we ignore the signals, the signs get louder, and the subconscious takes over and gets our attention through the body, whether it be aches and pains, disease or something more serious.

In her book The Anatomy of the Spirit, Caroline Myss cites an example of one of her clients, a dentist, who admitted that he 'hated his job to death' and it was causing him serious physical illness. Even when he was presented with evidence to show the link between hating his job and his ill health, he chose to remain because he prioritised money and the perceived status. Within 12 months, the dentist had died. An extreme case, but haven't you heard someone say, or have you uttered yourself, "My job is killing me"? Perhaps that's the time to take action, and definitely time to change your language about your career!

It's always seemed surprising to me how people spend so much of their lives unhappy at work, waiting to enjoy their time off. Those people are unhappy at work but then spend most of their leisure time complaining about work. Before you know it, 40 years have gone by, waiting for this perceived nirvana called retirement when they allow themselves to truly begin to enjoy their life. But unfortunately, by that stage, their health has deteriorated too much to do what they wanted to do.

If you want to see the effect your language can have on your body, watch a YouTube video on Dr Emoto's rice & water experiments. It shows how energetically powerful our words alone are. In this experiment, he puts rice and water into three beakers. For one month, he says 'thank you' to the first beaker, 'you're an idiot' to the second beaker, and he completely ignores the third beaker. The results: the rice in the first beaker thrived, the rice in the second beaker turned black, and the rice in the third beaker rotted completely.

Sadly, statistics show if you retire without any purpose or meaning, your life expectancy is six to seven years. How frightening is that? To work all your life towards having the freedom to enjoy it, and then you only have six or seven years to cram in everything you've wanted to do, assuming your health permits. That is also assuming you make it off the work treadmill without having a breakdown or heart attack from stress. And if you're one of those Type A personalities who is driven, driven, driven (did I mention driven?) and convince yourself that it's all worth it because you're doing it for your family, stop and take a look around. How connected are you to your family right now? Extrapolate that out by another ten years and imagine how life will be if nothing changes.

Sorry to be this blunt so early in the relationship! But if you're feeling like you want to throw this book down in anger or frustration, ask yourself why you feel angry or frustrated? You might not be aware of this pattern in your life, but if something annoys or triggers us about a situation, it's probably because there's a grain of truth in it for us that we do not want to recognise.

There's Another Way

I've spent most of my career like everyone else, working hard, trying to do the best job I can. I have to admit that the philosophy of "you have to work hard to achieve success" has never sat comfortably with me. After all, how many people do you know who work hard and are just getting by? When I hear people repeat this idea, the rebel inside me has always wanted to say, "I don't think that's true", I have an inner knowing that we can create the opposite of this. I have recently put this theory to the test, taking a step back in my business to create space in the last six months, and I'll talk about this in a later chapter. When we are busy being busy, we don't allow ourselves enough time to think about what we want or really observe what's going on in our lives. Perhaps that's why we keep ourselves so busy sometimes, because it's too hard to face the truth.

Taking time out to daydream about what we want and how life will be when we're living our dream is critical to us achieving what we want. Our thoughts create our reality, so we need to shape our thoughts. Getting into the right emotional state is essential to raising our vibration to attract experiences at the same vibration. So we have to believe it before we see it. We have to trust that we can attract what we want. I will show you how to do this with your career.

I'll leave you with this thought, you know there's something else inside of you, that's why you're attracted to this book. Think about how you will feel if you wait 10 or 20 years and haven't acted on this feeling. You've taken the first step by picking up this book, and you are well on your way to change already!

── CHAPTER 1 ──

AWAKEN: Recognising Wake-Up Calls

*If it was meant to be
Any other way,
It would have been*

[MATT KAHN]

When I became a Career Coach, my mantra was "to be that wake-up call for people before they have a serious wake-up call." I had worked in the recruitment industry for over 25 years and had seen the toll working in a high-pressure career had taken on many people. They might have been earning the big dollars, but their health and relationships were suffering as a result for many of them. When I went into career coaching, my initial focus was on wellbeing and making sure people were in a job that wouldn't negatively affect their health and happiness.

My personal experience in childhood had also made me determined to make sure people were happy in their careers. My Mum and Dad moved to Australia from England with three young children when I was one. Dad had been high up in the police force and could not transfer across at the same level and couldn't afford to start from scratch supporting a family of 5. Luckily, he was also very good at math, so he took a job in an accounting department in a large retail store, but he wasn't happy. Imagine going from working 'on the beat' and being in charge to being stuck behind a desk and answering to someone else. He had enormous pressure on him to provide for the family, and this took him into a career he didn't enjoy so that he could make ends meet. What you suppress, you have to express, and when he came home from work, he would let out his frustration. Living in that environment watching the impact on him, my Mum, and our family made me want to do something about it. I grew up questioning, "Why can't he just be happy?" and "Why does he have to be that way?"

For me, over time and having tuned into and followed my soul purpose, I now understand that it's not just about being happy for most of us. It's far greater than that. We have a knowing that there's more to this career stuff than what we were told when we were young. Although you might be able to do many different things, it's not just about what you can do; it's about what you truly want to do. Some of us grew up learning that we should be very grateful if someone offers us a job and should take it. I often see this programming when clients keep taking the wrong positions and come to me because they don't know how to say 'no' graciously. We know something is missing in our career, and we have gifts and talents we want to bring to life and make a difference in the world. That could be why you're reading this book. You've become conscious that you're here for a reason.

Before I share my path to my career awakening, I want to touch on the significance of experiencing challenges in our careers, such as having our role made redundant, receiving a poor performance review, or being passed over for a promotion. Sometimes it's not pleasant to reflect on these experiences because they often bring up feelings of pain, embarrassment, shame or resentment. However, they are vital to our awakening.

Career wake-up calls come into our lives for several reasons. We could be drifting off of our path and ignoring the signs, and the only way we pay attention is when something hits us like a sledgehammer, such as receiving a first warning, being made redundant or having a major health crisis. Whenever I work with people whose role has been made redundant, there comes a point where they confess they weren't happy there anyway and that it needed to happen.

Another reason career wake-up calls happen is that there could be a lesson we need to learn to progress and move along our path in life and prepare us for what's coming next. The challenge may arrive to shape us and equip us with the skills, gifts, and talents that we are here to share with the world. So we need to look for the clues. As I say, never waste a good crisis, but more about that in Chapter 2. For me, it was a 3-part process (some of us are more stubborn than others!)

I'm about to get real and share some not so proud moments in an otherwise successful career to show you what happens when we ignore the signs life gives us and how life works to help us get on our path. As I mentioned above, challenges are full of learnings, and I believe that my experiences make me a better career coach because I know what it's like when things don't go according to plan in our careers, plus I have a lived understanding. It's a bit of a long story but I find one of the best ways to teach is to provide real-life and relatable examples and it's in the spirit of sharing and helping you. So (gulp!) here goes!

Wake-up calls I ignored.

#1
Wake-up call

Looking back, I can pinpoint the exact decision I made that led to my first wake-up call. I'd been working with the same business owners for 18 years across two highly successful, international companies. I was selected to be one of three of their foundational team members to set up their start-up office in Adelaide. I'd had a consistently successful career across that time, always meeting and exceeding budgets for 18 years and building a team and contributing to a start-up business in a very competitive market. (Bear with me; I'm trying to build up some credibility here before I burst the bubble). From the outside, life looked good. Business life, that is, as I'd also just left my marriage, and at the same time, I was caring for my father, whose health declined rapidly, and within eight weeks, had passed away.

However, work-life was good. I led a successful team of about four consultants at the time, managed some major client accounts, and had performed consistently well. I can remember sitting back in my chair and thinking, "I like the clients I'm working with, so I'm just going to focus on them and make life simple." I wasn't going to waste time chasing businesses that already had strong relationships with other recruiters. It took a lot of time and effort to try and win them over, often with very little return on investment. Big mistake! The Universe doesn't like it when we get comfortable in life. After all, we're here to learn, grow, expand and challenge ourselves. Shortly after making this decision, the Global Financial Crisis (GFC) hit, and just about every organisation worldwide spiraled into downsizing, letting staff go. Very few of them were actively recruiting, especially the industries I'd decided to look after. Across the business nationally, consultants' billings plummeted, including mine. Fortunately, our Directors were very gracious. The lovely Geoff Morgan and Andrew Banks (you might know Andrew as one of the Shark Tank judges) made the universal decision to look after their staff during this rough time and freeze budgets to stop Consultants from falling into deficits.

So, where's the wake-up call?

After carrying a mindset of "there's no work out there" and "nothing's working" for a good 12-18 months after the impact of the GFC, I became stuck in this negative mindset. Although I was taking action, it was impossible to succeed when my mind told me nothing was working. Perception became projection. My team was managing okay, but I was recruiting roles paying over $100,000, and they were rare at that time. Then we had a change of General Manager who assessed everyone with a fresh set of eyes, and I imagine by this time had a plan to trim back those who had not managed to rebuild their billings. It was at this point a few of us received first warnings. The shame hit me like a tonne of bricks. It was like watching a horror movie. Work was everything to me, where I felt empowered, valued and successful. I loved my work! However, I do have to admit that I'd become comfortable, even bored at some points, and perhaps I hadn't taken any proactive action to leave because I didn't know what else I could do. I'd been doing well for so long, I think deep down, I doubted my ability to be good at anything else. I'd attributed my success to just doing the same thing for so long and having developed a good reputation. Little did I know it at the time, but one of my core limiting beliefs was holding me back. I'll talk more about that in Chapter 3.

You see, before the GFC, I'd had a desire to start my own business, but to do something different to recruitment. I'd already had the vision and passion for three years but hadn't taken a lot of action to get it up and running. I'd developed a business plan and a website, kidding myself that I was on my way, but I never took any steps to talk to people about it or commercialise it. It was just a hobby. I want you to hear what I'm saying here because it's important. *I'd been shown the path forward, but I ignored it.* What happens when we ignore our path and get off track? A challenge comes along to nudge us back onto our path, and usually, these external challenges aren't nice! I could have taken the courageous step and backed myself, but when I received the first warning, fear set in and as a single mum with a mortgage and my kids in a private school, I felt panicked to secure another job.

Here's where choices come in. You might be reading this and thinking, "Ruth, you're going through a divorce, your father has just passed away, and you're on the brink of losing your job. Give yourself a break. That's not the right time to start a business!" Or you might be thinking; you've chosen for your kids to go to a private school, take them out (trust me, I tried, but my ex-husband and I weren't on the same page with that). Nonetheless, we always have choices. Mistake #1: fear-based decision.

2
Wake-up call

After choosing to leave my previous role, I then transitioned into a Business Development Manager role with a small company. It was a newly created position working with a sole practitioner in the careers space. It was an excellent opportunity to leverage my recruitment and business development experience and pivot into something slightly different, and I was excited to learn something new. Knowing what I knew about business development, I thought it would take me 9-12 months to build new relationships and convert business. However, my employer was new to recruiting anyone in this capacity, and she expected to see a return on investment within three months. As we both later discovered, the reality was that it was more like 18 months.

We both set off with a strong feeling that things were going well, some business was coming in, we developed a new Executive Onboarding program together, and I was also assisting with program delivery and contributing ideas along the way. "If you can't do it,

Ruth, no-one can" were the words I went away at Christmas hearing her say, but when we came back in the New Year, those words had changed to "If you can't make it happen in the next three months Ruth, your job will be gone." I was in shock. What had happened? Perhaps a close examination of projected cash flow over Christmas raised concerns, and being a small business operator, I understand that she needed to make these decisions quickly. Trust me, though, I wasn't this calm and rational about it at the time.

So, this was opportunity number two to finally step out on my own and get my business up and running. If anything, working for a small business had shown me how you can convert ideas into services, and I knew how to market them. But no. Yet again, I opted to ignore my path and look for another paid position instead. Mistake # 2: comfort-based decision

#3
Wake-up call

Stepping out of recruitment for a while had allowed me to appreciate what I loved about it—talking to businesses about what makes them tick, their culture, their workforce, and what talent they needed—talking to people about what they wanted to do and finding them great opportunities. I loved problem-solving and using creative solutions to find people, and staying in touch with people once I'd placed them, and being their external sounding board. So when the opportunity arose to step back into recruitment with an organisation with a solid reputation in the Adelaide market, I grabbed it. I could actually see myself working there before I went for the interview, and with a strong endorsement from a friend who worked in the business, I got the job. Even though I had many years of recruitment experience, there were still a lot of challenges. I stepped into an existing team of six consultants that already had the market stitched up and had a better network than me at the Executive level. How was I going to get clients? When I went for the interview, the owner said to me, "Ruth, it doesn't matter how much experience you've had. It will take you 18 months to build your business here." And he was right, much to my frustration.

I loved reporting to the owner. He was incredibly successful, and he was a great sounding board, and I learnt a lot from him. All was going great until the owner changed the structure, and my role merged into the rest of the team, and I was suddenly reporting to someone with who I'd been in competition with from time to time over the years. My operating style was very different to his. I'd operated very autonomously, and his team worked very collaboratively. I thought I was saving everyone's time by not including them in my emails and keeping them informed of everything I was doing. Needless to say there were a few teething problems, and I had the feeling I was never going to be seen as a valuable team member. Finally, the penny dropped, and I'd learnt something from the first few wake-up calls. It was time. Time to pursue my dream and go out on my own. How many wake-up calls did I need after all?

I didn't know exactly what I wanted to do at this point, so I set off to take a weekend personal development course run by my first ever personal trainer, Michael Johnson, at the time he was known as 'The Mojo Master', to gain some clarity. It had taken me a while to sign up because I'd only known Michael as a PT, and at that time, he was young and very focused on himself, plus he was working across two jobs and wasn't 100% happy, and my perception was I didn't know what he could teach me. However, I attended a one-day seminar he'd run a few weeks earlier and saw how much he'd turned his life around and built a successful business, so I signed up for the weekend course. Three days of figuring out what was getting in the way of starting my own business, finding out what my kryptonite was and discovering my purpose. You can probably guess what was getting in my way - me of course.

There were two profound exercises we did over the weekend that impacted me. The first was getting clear on my values and purpose. When I wrote down my values: Careers, Health and Growth and then kept asking myself, "What is my purpose?" while I was looking at those words, Creating Healthy Careers came into my head and brought a smile to my face and lit me up inside. That night I registered the business and domain names.

It was the exercise on the last day that kicked me into action. We'd been writing down all the excuses that we make for not taking action in our lives and all the negative thoughts and limiting beliefs we had about ourselves. Michael dimmed the lights, played some dramatic music, got us standing up, holding onto our list of limiting beliefs, and future paced us. "If you hold onto these limiting beliefs and nothing changes, picture how life will look and feel in 12 months. In 3 years. In 5 years. In 10 years." Like everyone else in the room, I was crying hysterically by this stage. Thank God the lights were out. I was 50 at the time, and it hit me. Ten years goes by so fast. If I don't' take action now, those ten years will go by, and how will I feel looking back at my life knowing that I didn't give it a go after holding onto this dream for so long. If I didn't take a chance, didn't back myself, didn't listen to that inner whisper. What role model would I be to my kids? How could I live with myself? Suddenly the fear of not doing it, not starting my own business, was greater than the fear of doing it.

By the end of the weekend, I'd signed up to do three consecutive coaching courses, and by the end of the year (about six months later), I'd resigned and started my business.

I knew people would probably think I was crazy leaving a perfectly good job without any other financial support to start my business while having shared responsibility for two children. The ideal would have been to build a business on the side, get the income ramped up and then move across. There were two reasons I didn't take this approach. The first one was because I didn't want to do it that way. I felt like my energy would be split between two jobs, and I wouldn't succeed at either, plus it would be a slow process, and I felt ready now! The second reason was that ethically I couldn't remain in my 'day job' while providing the services I needed to in my business as my boss would have perceived there to have been a conflict. This just reinforced my desire to quit and start cold turkey. My validation came when I attended a Job Expo and Janine Allis, the founder of Boost Juice, spoke on a panel. At the end of her presentation, I jumped up and stood with a small group at the front of the room, waiting for my turn to catch her attention because I felt sure she was going to confirm my thinking based on her own story and how she'd started her very successful business. "You've got to go all-in" she said, "You can't have a foot in both camps." This time I was ready to hear this advice. I was seeking that endorsement. Several years earlier, when I was reading "Think and Grow Rich" by Napoleon Hill, I remember shutting the book and putting it away for years when I got to the part about burning all bridges behind you so that there was only one way forward. I shut it because I knew it was what I needed to do, but I wasn't brave enough to do it at that point in my life. I didn't have the courage to back myself and take a risk. It's interesting how the right thoughts and information present themselves when you are ready to hear them.

Several years earlier, I attended a business breakfast and sat next to one of my former General Managers. We were catching up and discussing our plans, and I commented, "Sometimes I just think I should sell my house to fund going into my own business." The words came out of my mouth, but I didn't know where they came from. It was a bold statement, and it was a desire that was within me, and for some reason, that morning, it decided to rise to the surface and come to life through my words, or a declaration as it turned out to be.

Little did I know that I was breathing this statement into reality. They say watch what you wish for, and I have truly learnt the power of our thoughts creating our reality, however we don't always know what events will transpire to bring our desires into being, but I was about to find out.

Amid undertaking my coaching qualifications, funds were running out. As I mentioned, I'd been through a divorce, was paying child support and paying private school fees and a mortgage – all on one income. What was I going to do?

Lying in bed one night, I was unable to sleep and was stressed because I only had enough money in my account to last me the next two months. That earlier thought came back to me, "What if I sold my house to fund me going into business?" The house next to mine had just sold and was identical to mine. What if I reached out to the same real estate agent to see if she had any potential purchasers still interested? So I did. The following day we met and negotiated a contract. The agent brought three couples through, and I received two offers. The following night I was signing the sale contract. I'd sold the house within three days and hadn't even put it on the market! Everything lined up. Then I realised, "Oh shit, now I better start the business, or that money will disappear, and I would have missed my chance", so I did.

Now I don't advocate that everyone sells their house and gamble it all on a dream. What I'm saying is that we all have choices. I had a friend who wasn't happy in her job, and every time I saw her, we would have a conversation about work and how unhappy she was. I'd suggested a potential pathway to her, but it meant taking a drop in income in the short term, and at the time, she didn't want to sacrifice her overseas holidays. She made her choice!

I love the expression that when you follow your path, the Universe will have your back, and as I write this book, I'm no millionaire (yet), but I know there is truth to this saying. There have been several times in my life when I've made big, life-changing decisions and then been wracked with doubt but have had an inner whisper give me reassurance or a nudge in the right direction. About six months into my business, the adrenalin had worn off, the money wasn't coming in, and things were getting quite stressful. It felt like I was on the brink of depression. I was on my morning beach walk this particular windy winter morning, listening to a podcast as I did each morning, and I decided to take the earplugs out and just listen to the ocean. As I walked, I wondered why things weren't going to plan. I felt like I'd put everything on the line to pursue my purpose, so why wasn't everything falling into place? Then that trusty little voice entered my head and said, "You wouldn't have been placed on this path to fail." I took this as a sign to trust. Trust that the Universe had my back. Trust that I was on my path. Trust that it would all work out. I am now entering my 5th year in business as I write this, so I'm glad I trusted. If I'd have known then where that path was going to take me, doing theta healing, using intuitive healing methods, even clearing generational and past life beliefs, I would have said "who, me?". But just like that walk, it's taking one step and then another, and you get there.

So there you go, an introduction to my world. You might now be thinking, "why on earth would I take career advice from someone who has had so many wake-up calls in their career?" Trust me, would you want coaching from someone who hasn't navigated challenges in their career? People come to coaches when they want help navigating problems, challenges and road blocks, and as a coach, I feel my value proposition to my clients is strengthened by my lived experience. Having experienced what I have enables me to relate to what many of my clients are dealing with. When I share, they feel comfortable opening up. My experiences have guided me to develop tools and strategies that have worked for me and now work for my clients, and help them avoid unnecessary wake-up calls. And as you will discover, we have to go through this to help us develop the skills we need to help us live our purpose.

So, where are you in the process of your wake-up calls? Are you paying attention? Asking why these experiences are coming into your life? Has anything I've said resonated with you? Are you ready to take this journey and see what your life has shown you about your career?

Notes:

Notes:

© Creating Healthy Careers 2022

Notes:

─── **CHAPTER 2** ───

EXPANSION:
Learning What Life's Lessons Have Shown You About Your Soul Purpose

*It all depends on how
we look at things,
And not how they are in themselves.*

[CARL JUNG]

I can remember years ago, as I was going through my divorce, I said to the Universe, "Okay, I've learnt enough. No more challenges, please". Little did I realise at that stage the purpose and benefit of challenges.

Since then, I've invested a lot of time and energy into personal and professional development, and I've uncovered the wisdom to view challenges differently and appreciate why they're in our lives and how they strengthen us. You may have heard the story about how the caterpillar transforms to a butterfly within the chrysalis, and an essential part of its transformation is when it's wings strengthen as it beats them against the wall of the chrysalis to break free. The resistance is essential to its growth.

What I've learnt is that one reason challenges come into our life is to show us when we have drifted off our path, or to equip us with skills, knowledge or insights to help us grow, as our journey here is to learn and expand. They contain clues of who we need to become.

Another pattern I have recognized lately is:

when we seek something outside of ourselves (love, security, validation, self-worth), the Universe will give us the opposite so that we have to develop that 'thing' or characteristic within ourselves.

It's all pointing us back to self-growth and expansion. There is beauty and gifts in our wounds, and we need to take the time to find them. These lessons are for our soul's highest good, to grow, learn and heal.

In this chapter, I will share some practical ways of obtaining the learnings and digging for the gold in your challenges, plus strategies to reframe and gain a different perspective and understanding of what's going on in your life and career.

Joining The Dots

This exercise can help us find the clues in our past, and join the dots to see what our challenges are showing us about the gifts, talents, knowledge we are here to develop, and how these challenges shape our career purpose.

Steve Jobs once said: "You can't connect the dots looking forwards; you can only connect them looking backwards. So you have to trust that the dots will somehow connect in the future."

This is as true for our careers as it is in our lives so let's see how this philosophy looks in real life.

For the early years in my career, I drifted from job to job, only lasting a year or two anywhere until I got bored and moved on. Then I seemingly stumbled into recruitment, and spent over 27 years in that industry. Four years ago I finally started to feel like I was really finding my path by moving my career into career coaching. The clues had always been there though. I'd always enjoyed talking to people who love what they do in their career and diving into their back story to understand what took them down that path. Ever since I started in the workforce, friends would gravitate towards me to open up about the issues they were having at work. I've always been a good listener and passionately believed that work should be something you enjoy, something that adds to your life. On top of that, my childhood experience gave me a focus on wanting people to be happy in their job. So it shouldn't come as a huge surprise that I moved into coaching people to find happiness and success in their careers. I've heard it said that your voids create your values, which means what is lacking in your life when you're young, becomes important to you as you get older, and I can see that's precisely how Creating Healthy Careers came to be on the top of my list!

Let's dig a bit deeper here and show you how to identify and join the dots in your life.

There were three key influencers in my childhood who all brought something very different into my life: my Dad, my Grandad and my Mum.

Let me paint a picture of how Creating Healthy Careers all came to be and the 'dots' or stepping stones that brought me to where I am now.

I mentioned in Chapter 1 about my Dad and how his career transition from the Police Force to an accounts department impacted his happiness and our home life. The other side of that story was that Mum and Dad were always getting ill with one thing or another, and my mother unfortunately passed away very early in life, at the age of 63. I've since learned a lot about psychosomatics (the mind/body connection and how thoughts impact us at a cellular level); and I think all of that stress took a toll on her health as she tried to buffer us children from Dad's frustrations. When we suppress emotions and push them down, they ultimately manifest physically. In other words, if you don't deal with what's going on in your life and release any negative emotions, your body will pay the price. Deepak Chopra talks about this mind-body connection in his book Perfect Health in his explanation of quantum physics where thoughts are instantly felt within the cells in our body.

Dot # *1*

My lesson from Dad was that you need to be happy in your career, no matter what you're doing. Otherwise, it negatively impacts your relationships, family, health, and self-worth.

Dot # *2*

On the other hand, my grandfather had a very different perspective. He had grown up in foster care in England during WW1 and had experienced extreme hardship. Yet he chose to have an attitude of gratitude. He was grateful for any opportunity he received in life, and he had a strong work ethic and was resilient. One of his many pearls of wisdom to me growing up was "never leave a bad smell wherever you go." He had such a way with words didn't he! My lesson from Grandad was to choose my thinking and focus on what makes me grateful. Even when I'm not happy in a job and have decided that it's time to move on, I find something that I enjoy and try to shift my focus to that.

Dot # 3

Then there was my gorgeous Mum. Mum's lesson to me was to love what you do and that it's never too late to find the career you want.

Mum was one of those people that everybody loved. She was warm and lovable and never spoke negatively about anyone. Mum had put her career on hold while raising the family. Clearly family was a high value for her as she adopted and raised three toddlers aged 1, 2 and 3! Many years later, when the three of us were all independent, Mum then wanted to get back into the workforce. Having also been in the police force, Mum pursued her interest in social justice and aligned her career with a related industry, retail security, which enabled her to work flexible hours to still be there for her family. She also grew to follow in Grandad and Grandma's footsteps, becoming very good at lawn bowls and pursued a leadership role much later in life, becoming the South Australian Women's President. She'd carved out a career doing what she loved.

So why Creating Healthy Careers? To help people align their passion with their profession so that they live a life of purpose, do what they love and so that their career adds to their health and doesn't detract from it. Dots joined!

So it's now your turn. It's essential to take time out and look for the clues in your life. When you venture down this path to discovering your personal genius, be prepared to embody it. I have guided many people to reach the point of clarity and for a moment they get excited about how their life could be, and then let fear and doubt stop them stepping into it and ultimately reject their power. So I will give you two pieces of advice at this point. Firstly, acknowledge that it is normal for fear to show up at this stage and once again, is simply the subconscious trying to keep you playing it small and safe. Secondly, ask yourself, when you realise everyone and everything that has been orchestrated to bring these gifts and talents into your life, who are you to turn your back on them and not bring them into the world? That statement has given me the courage to move forward in the face of fear once I'd seen what I was here to do, and not let my self-doubt stop me.

Over to you. Create a quiet space to reflect on the following questions:

Join The Dots Exercise

Who were the three prominent key influencers in your life when you were younger who shaped your beliefs and interests? What lessons were they in your life to teach you?

....

....

....

....

What are the three most defining moments in your childhood (good or bad), and what were the lessons you learnt?

....
....
....
....
....

What has your life story revealed to you?

....
....
....
....

What have been some of the significant life experiences/ challenges that have impacted your life, made you change direction or challenged you? What do you think they came into your life to teach you/guide you to do?

....
....
....
....
....

Have a look back at your life and see what has consistently brought you energy, what has lit you up, what was present?

....

....

....

....

....

When you reflect on the jobs you've thrived in, take a minute to look back, join the dots, and identify the consistent threads. What have been the key ingredients to a thriving work environment for you?

....

....

....

....

....

Everything in our life is meaningful, and I've found that I have shifted from feeling powerless to empowered by looking for the meaning in situations and challenges. Here are some other perspectives to view the bumps in the road in your career that may also provide clues about who you are here to become and how you are here to serve.

Reframe # 1
What is this situation in my life to teach me or strengthen in me?

It is essential to find the gold in circumstances that have happened in our career or life by asking this question. It helps shift focus from blame (helplessness) to taking responsibility for our life. We're digging for gold.

Reframing helps us change our perspective on past circumstances and stop us from harboring negative emotions that can keep us stuck in the past. Just like when you completed the Join the Dots exercise and identified some major life-changing events, and saw them through the lens of how they helped shape your career and values. When you actually 'get' the hidden message in the experience, it will give you a feeling of enlightenment.

For example, as a result of watching my father create a stressful atmosphere at home growing up, I had held negative feelings towards him for most of my life until I saw what he brought into my life from a different perspective. If these relationships are fated meetings, then what was he in my life to teach me? First, my purpose, helping people on their path so they'll be happy and healthy in their careers, for them and their family's benefit. Second, having him in my life made me develop characteristics of independence, strength and resilience. And third, if it weren't for him, I may not have developed my curiosity about understanding people and human behaviour. My Dad shaped me and my life in many other ways, and I've reached a stage of appreciation for most of them now. Some I'm still working on.

When I coach people, what's showing up in their careers can be an insight into something going on in their lives. Our programming and beliefs inform how we respond in and out of work. So it's not surprising that when we take a look under the hood at work, it connects with something that's happened in our personal lives too.

© Creating Healthy Careers 2022

Reframe # 2
Choose Your Challenges

If you are not on your path in life and are not taking action, life will let you know. We are all here to grow and expand and typically this occurs when we are out of our comfort zone. If you've become too comfortable and are not challenging yourself in your career, you will get feedback, either externally (from people around you) or internally (within your body). Your performance may start to decline; your boss will notice, and then, here comes a nudge or wake-up call to get your attention.

We need to pay attention to these little nudge's or wake up calls while they are only minor, because if we ignore the little signs, have you ever noticed that the signs tend to get bigger?

Arianna Huffington's story shows just how we tend to turn a blind eye to the little signs, until we can't ignore them anymore. Arianna runs Huffington Post in the US, a wildly successful publication, and she now writes on wellbeing. Arianna pushed herself so hard early in her career that she collapsed while working from home. As she fell, she hit her head on the corner of her desk and was knocked unconscious. The question she asked herself when she came to was, "how did I not realise I was so run down?"

So how can we avoid having one of these wake-up calls? I was recently reminded that when we put all our effort into one area of our life and don't focus on having some balance, life will soon bring it to our attention. Just before Christmas I was talking to someone saying how I'd just completed my strategic planning for the next year and felt good about where I was heading. Then they asked me, "And what about your relationship?". "Ah, what relationship?" I asked. I realized that I needed to start focusing on some other areas of my life, and not get totally absorbed with my business, as life had been a bit lopsided, so this was a good reminder. I pulled out my

Expansion

Wellbeing Wheel (below) to check which areas of my life were a little out of balance. I'd been focusing on career, finances, spiritual development, mindset and purpose. However, relationships and physical wellbeing needed some attention. I then looked at which one I needed to prioritise, and it was physical wellbeing for me.

Have a look at the wheel and mark in each area on a scale of 1 to 10 where you are. Then identify which areas you want to focus on now and write down what action can you take to improve that area of your life:

Wellbeing Wheel

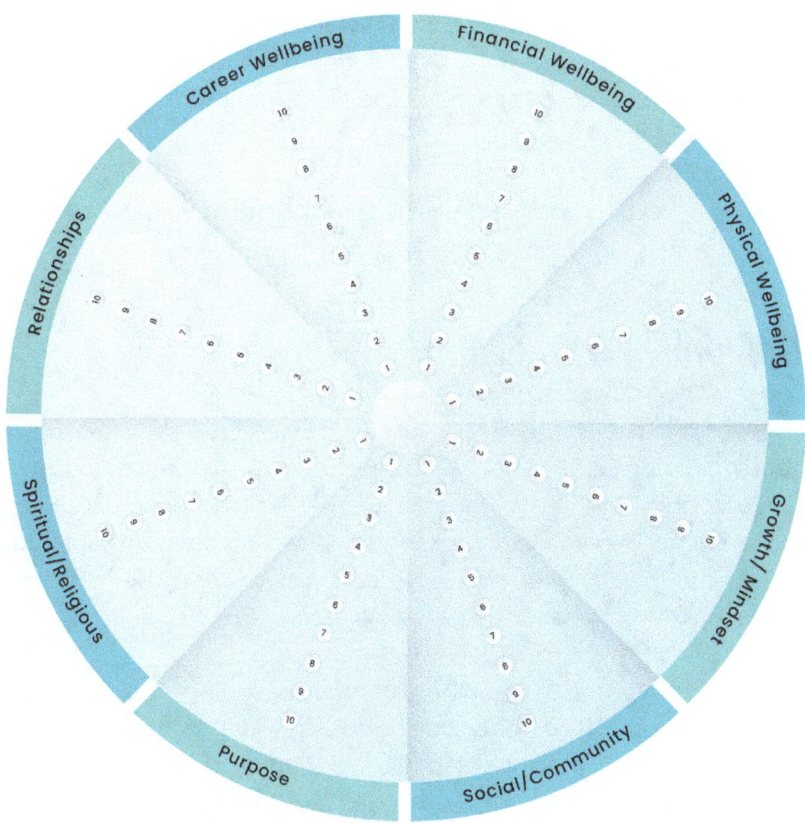

> » Put a cross in each section to mark your level of satisfaction from 1-10.
> » Draw a line joining all the crosses.
> » Which areas will have the biggest impact on improving your wellbeing?
> » Think about the impact your career is having on the other areas.

Reframe # 3
If It Was Meant To Be Any Other Way, It Would Have Been

This one came from Matt Kahn, a spiritual teacher and healer "If it was meant to be any other way, it would have been". I love it and find that it gives people a sense of acceptance of what's going on. It almost permits us to stop resisting 'what could have been' and accept what is.

It's simple, and I'm going to leave it at that. Remind yourself of it the next time something doesn't go your way.

Reframe # 4
The Bus Stop Conversation

Reading Dr Sue Morter's book "The Energy Codes", I came across this analogy and have used it so many times to help people look for the learnings in perceived challenges. Please suspend any spiritual or religious beliefs you may have and just take on the insightful perspective it provides.

Dr Morter invites us to imagine that you are sitting at a bus stop before you enter this world, waiting for your journey to begin. You are thinking about what you'd like to learn or develop this time around. "This time, I want a level 10 experience in acceptance and forgiveness", and you ask the others at the bus stop, "Who's going to help me?". Someone at the bus stop offers to help. Off you both go on your journey without knowing how it's going to happen. Then one day you're driving along and a car crashes into you, a drunk driver. It's the person from the bus stop who's come to give you an experience to help you learn how to accept and forgive. Wow, how's that for a reframe!

We can use the bus stop conversation to take responsibility for what happens in our lives and look into why we would have asked for it to happen and what we wanted to develop or learn. Once again it flips our perspective from focusing on the negative, to look for the positive.

And one final reframe, remember, when you learn the lesson, the lesson will disappear! There is no longer a need for the lesson to keep showing up in your life. Ever notice how you think you are leaving a problem behind when you change jobs, only to find it surfaces in the next job, or the next one?

Allowing yourself to reflect on your life's experiences and challenges through the lens of "what is the learning that I need to gain from this?" will give you a newfound appreciation and sense of gratitude for what you have experienced. It will also give you insights into the skills, knowledge and wisdom you have to share with the world.

Throughout these experiences, you would have also formed and filed away some limiting beliefs that may be holding you back in your career. So in the next chapter, we'll look at how to release any negative beliefs that may be causing blind spots in your career, and stopping you from walking your path.

© Creating Healthy Careers 2022

Notes:

Notes:

Notes:

— CHAPTER 3 —

CLEARING: Releasing What is Blocking Your Path

The only limits in your life are the ones you create in your mind!

[NAPOLEON HILL]

I love the story about when Michelangelo was asked how he created the statue of David, and his response was that he just chipped away everything that wasn't David.

When we can chip away all the things that aren't truly us, and that are getting in the way of us being our true selves, we can then step into the life we are here to live.

So let's start chipping!

Are your Beliefs Running the Show?

Yes! As I mentioned earlier, our subconscious mind is running the show in our lives, so to change our external world, we need to change our inner world, including reprogramming our subconscious mind. Did you know that approximately 90% of our decisions and actions come from the subconscious mind, and our conscious mind is only in control 10% of the time? It makes sense because we don't consciously do things to achieve negative results in our life, do we?

You may be thinking (and if you are, it's probably your subconscious mind talking to you), "Well, we can't do anything about that. It's our subconscious mind, and it runs on autopilot." Yes, that's true, but ask yourself, who programs the autopilot? We do. We've done it very effectively for most of our lives, and so now we are going to reprogram it in the same way we've always done, through our thoughts and self-talk.

The book A Course In Miracles (ACIM) suggests, "when you change your thoughts of the past, you change your thoughts of the future, and thus create a better future." So when you change your perception around past experiences that may be keeping you stuck in the past, you can free yourself up to create something new. We can often hold ourselves back in our careers because of a limiting belief formed as a child. "I'm not smart enough", or "I don't deserve to be happy" or "good things just don't happen for me". You can imagine that once you can view the past from a different perspective, perhaps appreciating that it was a throwaway comment from an adult that didn't have anything to do with you that resulted in your belief, it can free you to go after what you truly want in your career.

When a pattern starts to form, and the same things keep happening in our career, or the same challenging people keep popping up, we need to stop and realise that the common factor is us, and that's a good thing to recognise because then it is within our power to do something about it. It can be tough to accept that fact, but that awareness is the start of working out what's going on and stopping what's blocking us from achieving what we want to in our careers. When we dig under the surface, we see that these blocks are our programs or our limiting beliefs occurring subconsciously, and that's why we are blind to them until we stop and pay attention.

It's also essential to clear these old beliefs if we want to attract or create something new in our lives because you attract what you are, so we need to shift ourselves and our perspective of ourselves into that person we want to become. By the end of this book, you will have a strong sense of why you are here and how your life has shaped you, and you will be on the path to becoming the person you want to be.

But let's start by understanding what beliefs are and how they form, to stop the same patterns from repeating in your career, and get a clear sight of your blind spots.

Beliefs are stored in the subconscious part of the mind and are your own personal 'playbook' based on lessons learnt earlier in our life, to move us away from any danger and stop us from repeating mistakes.

Typically our beliefs, or programs, are formed between the ages of 0 – 7, and in fact, we can inherit certain beliefs as well, generationally and historically. Their fundamental purpose is to keep us safe. There would have been a time in your life when something happened you perceived to be dangerous or hurtful, and you made a decision to avoid feeling that way again. A typical illustration of this process often occurs at school. Perhaps we put up our hand to answer a question and were laughed at by the class. At that moment, we might have felt so much pain that we decided we weren't going to speak up again or that it's not safe to put our point of view forward. You can see how our belief is trying to protect us, but there comes a point when this belief no longer serves us later in life. At work, for example, when our opinion is sought by our boss, colleagues, and clients, but we feel unsafe to express it—the belief is now getting in our way. As a result, we miss out on job opportunities, winning business or promotions. I had one client who was so scared to speak up as a result of bullying in the workplace that she developed IBS (irritable bowel syndrome) because the suppression of her thoughts, feelings and emotions was literally making her sick to the stomach. When we corrected the cause, the symptoms eased.

You can see how important it is to identify when these beliefs or blocks are at play. One way to notice them is to determine when patterns start to form in your career or life.

This doesn't mean relinquishing responsibility and blaming our upbringing or other external factors. We all make choices throughout our lives; however, by understanding some of the beliefs, programs, or filters that we see life through, we create awareness, and when we have an understanding, we can make different choices.

You may have heard the phrase "perception is projection", in other words, what you perceive is happening is what you are projecting into the outside world. Then, people and events that resonate with that perception present themselves. Taking a look at the neuroscience behind this, we have what's known as the Reticular Activating System (RAS) in our subconscious mind, which acts as a filter. Our beliefs are filed away in the RAS, and it takes in information that's congruent with our beliefs. The RAS can't actually discern whether a belief is true or not, and it just accepts them as being the truth. It then sifts through the information presented to the mind and, because our mind can't process every bit of information it is exposed to, it then sorts through what it needs to know. It seeks evidence to validate our beliefs, and then in many cases, you end up creating and attracting events in your life to prove your beliefs. Hence, your thoughts become your reality. From a spiritual perspective, as I've mentioned previously, the same lessons will keep showing up in our lives until we get the learning, or grow or develop what we need to within us, then we break the cycle.

There are three things we want to do to set ourselves free from these limiting beliefs:

» Firstly, clean the lens – identify and reprogram beliefs

» Secondly, obtain the learnings from the challenges we have experienced in our life so that the lesson doesn't need to keep presenting itself (discussed in Chapter 2)

» Thirdly, we need to install a new picture or program of how we want life to look to keep sending the unconscious mind a visual of what it needs to search for in life, to help reprogram the RAS (through visualisation).

Identify And Reprogram Beliefs

As I've touched on above, one way to identify if a belief is running the show is to see whether there is an unwanted recurring pattern in your life. That's your blind spot! It's your belief that's directing your thought traffic. So when you find yourself getting frustrated because something keeps happening to you, and find yourself asking "why does this keep happening?", stop and look into the situation. What's triggering you, and what are you feeling and thinking. Keep digging.

Another indicator might be that you're stuck and not taking action. Ask yourself this question:

Is there any fear around me stepping into my dream career and following my path?

Pay attention to how your body and especially your gut, responds. In Theta Healing, we use muscle testing to see how the body responds to different statements. It's the same in kinesiology. There is an instantaneous connection between the brain and your body's cells (quantum physics has proven how this connection works subconsciously). Your biochemistry will react and tell you what's going on, this is where the expression 'gut feel' comes from.

If fear underlies any decision, your mind will not make available to you the steps you need to take to achieve that goal. You need to identify what the underlying belief or fear is. What are you scared of?

Ask yourself a series of questions starting with "what's the worst thing that would happen if I got my dream job?". Then repeatedly ask "and then what, and then what, and then what, and what would happen then?" Keep going until you say something that evokes an emotional reaction. You'll know you've hit on it. Then ask yourself the question, "what would not happen if I got my dream job?" It might be that people in your life are looking after you, supporting you, and you're scared you might lose their attention and support if you were happy in your job and all was well in your life. Safety and security are often big motivators to hold onto a belief. If you keep digging, you might find your mind is linking getting a new job to death! Surprising I know, but death underpins many fears at the core when you get down to the bottom belief. Let me show you how the mind makes this connection: you could fail, lose your job, lose your home, be out on the streets, get sick and die. These aren't conscious thoughts, but they're in there, under the surface. Aren't we interesting creatures! Becoming aware of what's going on will be a big step towards clearing that old limiting belief.

When I started coaching people to identify their career purpose, I noticed a pattern. They'd identify what they'd love to do, but then all the hidden fears, self-doubt, limiting beliefs, and excuses would come up and stop them from taking action, which is why it took me seven years to start my business. So I had to find a tool to help people get these beliefs out of the way.

That's when I came across Theta Healing, which features a very effective digging process to identify the bottom belief. We then create the new belief the client would like installed and use theta healing (which involves getting into a meditative state) to observe the new program taking shape in their lives. We then muscle test to ensure the body and mind has accepted the new belief. Once the subconscious has accepted the new belief, it works as described earlier in the RAS to help you see, create and attract events in line with it. It's fascinating. I love it and have had some fascinating results using it. For over a decade, one client consistently acquired different illnesses and didn't know why. When we drilled down to the bottom belief, we discovered that when she was at school, she was one of the intelligent kids in class and would get bullied when she performed well. She started to fake being ill so she could stay at home. Her subconscious had stored that highly effective strategy away, and whenever she began to do well in her career, get a new job, get a promotion, she'd get ill. This is how powerful beliefs can be in our lives! Another client had her own business and was already reasonably successful and wanted to grow her business further but kept hitting a ceiling. She was always fearful that there might not be enough money to support her family as she was the key bread winner. Underpinning her success was a mindset of scarcity that linked back to childhood, watching her entrepreneurial father experience extreme highs and lows. The hidden belief was that as soon as she started making money, she would lose it, so we corrected this belief with a new view that she was worthy of abundance and it was safe to expand her business.

One of the beliefs that stopped me from stepping up in my career was that I was stupid. I'd heard it often growing up "what would you know? You're just a stupid little girl." So whenever an opportunity came up to take on a leadership role, for many years, I resisted. You can imagine the resistance when I wanted to go into my own business, "Who do you think you are?". No wonder it took me seven years! One thing that helped me was to look for evidence in my life where I had achieved something, and where people had witnessed it (to ensure I wasn't just making it up in my mind), which validated my worth and my intelligence. I had to use their belief in me until I cracked my inner belief. It took a while because it had become deeply embedded during those formative years.

Basically, at the root of all limiting beliefs is fear, and one thing I have learnt is that we need to take action in the face of fear, not necessarily eliminate fear from our lives. If we're feeling fear, it's most likely because we are pushing the boundaries outside of our comfort zone, which is incredible, so get excited when you feel fear. It means you are truly living your life, and amazing things can happen on the other side of fear. I have experienced many degrees of fear throughout my life and survived, and I felt exhilaration on the other side. From starting my life over as a single mum in my 40's, starting my business at 50, delivering training programs feeling extremely nervous and then feeling amazing at the end, coaching clients who have been challenging and then watching them have a breakthrough. I wouldn't have experienced those wonderful feelings if I'd waited for courage first and then taken action. It works the other way around!

I want to give you a few questions to help you identify and overcome some of your limiting beliefs while you go through this process.

The first thing to do is pay attention to what comes to mind after you make a decision that takes you out of your comfort zone.

Write down the self-talk coming up, as that is a clue into what is going on in the subconscious mind.

Then pick out the primary phrase that hits home. For me, it was "I'm just a stupid little girl."

Now, ask yourself, how is holding onto this belief serving you? (there must be a benefit or payoff, or your mind wouldn't still be using it).

....
....
....
....

What's the worst thing that would happen if you didn't have that belief? (this will uncover any reason you won't let it go).

....
....
....
....

Then write down how that belief has held you back in life so you can see the cost of holding onto it.

....
....
....
....
....
....

How will your life be in 10 years if you still hold onto that belief?

....

....

....

....

Now create a new belief that WILL serve you and write it down. As you say the new belief, give it an emotional charge as this will help anchor it into your subconscious mind and every cell of your body. You might also use your body to help express yourself as you say this new belief to really embed it. This then enhances its ability to transition from a thought into physical reality.

....

....

....

....

....

....

Every time you notice yourself saying the old belief, interrupt that pattern by saying something to yourself like 'Cancel' or 'Delete' or reassure your subconscious mind that you are safe to do something new. Then remind yourself of the new belief. This will feel a little uncomfortable at first, but that's because we're creating a new groove (or dirt road as I like to call it) in the neural pathways, and it takes a bit of extra energy to stop being on autopilot going down the old pathway, reverse and start in the new direction.

I'll let you in on a little life secret ...... it doesn't matter what the circumstances are that led us to form a belief. When other events in life trigger a similar emotion in us, they allow us to look into what's causing us to have that emotional charge and then release that emotion. If we keep revisiting the 'story' that triggered that emotion and ask why and 'where did it come from?' we keep re-activating and strengthening that belief and keeping it present in our life. As Esther & Abraham Hicks keep saying in their work on the Laws of Attraction: "A belief is simply a thought that we keep thinking." So, let's change the thought. People often change jobs to move away from the perceived problem, only to find that the problem has followed them. You can change the external world, but nothing changes until you change the inner world.

What new beliefs can you choose?

As the subconscious is programmed through repetition, we can correct the programming through repetition. Affirmations or autosuggestion can work in many cases. Sometimes, just becoming aware of the belief and bringing it from the subconscious into the conscious can shine a light on it and dissolve it.

I know at this point you might be thinking, "That's all airy-fairy stuff". I would have agreed with you until I started reading many books by highly successful people and found they all used affirmations as part of their success strategy. Hal Elrod, who wrote "The Miracle Morning", talks about connecting emotion to your affirmations. You'll hear Bob Proctor and Anthony Robbins (both globally successful coaches) advocate the same approach, and Tony amps up his sentiment by using the body as well to anchor the emotion. Napoleon Hill also talks about 'autosuggestion' in "Think and Grow Rich". So with all of these highly successful people saying the same thing (and remember, Napoleon Hill interviewed 500 of the world's most successful people to elicit their secrets to success), there must be something in it.

We want to engage emotions as we say affirmations so as to really start to feel that we're already living the statement we're making. Remember, new thoughts lead to new emotions/feelings, which lead to new actions that lead to new results. As I mentioned earlier, our subconscious mind is programmed through repetition over many years. We do it all the time already; however, typically, we do it without realising that we're programming negative thoughts. So one effective way to reprogram it is to repeat the same thoughts, statements, and behaviours by consciously programming how you want things to be, and feeling and seeing things as if they are already that way. Bob Proctor, an amazing life success coach, starts it off by writing out his goals with, "I'm so happy and grateful now that ...." Notice it's in the present tense. Once you've written it and said it with emotion, hold that thought and feeling for 17 seconds so that your body has a chance to really connect with it.

If you believe that life is a struggle, which is what I carried around with me for most of my life, and success doesn't come easily, what do you think you will create in your career? A great affirmation to reprogram this with would be "success flows to me effortlessly" or "I am a magnet for success." Choose statements that give you a feeling of excitement. I had a boss once tell me early in my career, "everything you touch turns to gold", and it gave me a bulletproof mindset in that job that everything I took on would work out, and it did. I was working as a PA at the time but took on a resume business that hadn't been performing, and turned it around. I was quickly promoted into my first consulting role and got to travel the country and go to exciting places I would never have visited otherwise. Sometimes we'd be at a location over a weekend, so I got to combine a holiday with work and stay in lovely hotels, expenses paid. I met some fascinating people and, at the same time, honed my interview skills, which still serve me well today. That role then leveraged me to start my recruitment career, which lasted more than 27 years.

Install A New Picture

We can also reprogram the subconscious mind through visualisation. If we picture life going a certain way enough times in our conscious mind, it will filter through to our subconscious mind, change any opposing beliefs there, and ultimately lead to new actions and results. One time, I was upping my game in the recruitment industry and going for a job operating at a much more senior level. I visualised myself working in the office before I even went for the interview. When I went for the interview, I already felt like I worked there and was relaxed and confident in the interview. The outcome … I got the job. The opposite is also true. Think back to when you were learning to ride a bike. You'd be paranoid that you'd ride off the path and hit a tree or fence, so your focus was on the tree or fence, not the path you wanted to follow. The next minute, the bike would be veering off track toward the tree. So we want to keep our mind focused on where we want to go.

Visualisation is a great way to elicit feelings to bring you into vibrational alignment with the thing you want to achieve or acquire. Part of my morning routine includes writing out my main goals, then saying them with emotion, and then sitting and picturing that goal as if it was true until I feel how it would feel living it. Revisiting this vision throughout the day can help lift your feelings and then change the course of the action you take. Athletes use visualisation as an essential part of their training to see themselves achieving a successful outcome before their event. Have you ever noticed the divers standing at the top of the tower doing little body twists and turns before they dive? It's even been proven that spending time visualising yourself doing an exercise like weights can even impact your physiology and muscle growth without even stepping into the gym! So the power of visualisation is not to be underestimated.

Let's look at the influence of visualisation and its relationship with energy to see how we can use it to help our thoughts become our reality in our career. From a spiritual perspective, we have the understanding that our higher self is planting little seeds in our mind to show us what it wants us to achieve. This is why we shouldn't just dismiss thoughts or ideas that pop into our mind. They are there for a reason. However, I also find it is valuable for some people to have the scientific perception of what's happening as well. A fascinating experiment that demonstrates this was conducted by Thomas Young in 1801 called The Observer Affect or the Double Slit Experiment where he proved how a beam of electrons is affected simply by the act of being observed. This showed that particles behaved differently when someone was in the room observing the experiment compared to when the space was empty, proving the power of observation. In Theta Healing, as a practitioner, we are not doing the work; we are in the role of observing the healing for it to happen. So when you realise we live in an ocean of energy, all the thoughts, knowledge and ideas already exist as energy in this sea and it is the act of observing and visualising what we want that brings energy into form.

Have you ever had a time where you've thought of someone, and then within a short time, they've contacted you, or you've bumped into them? It happens to me all the time. In one instance, I had this random thought about a woman I hadn't seen for years as I was going for my morning walk down the beach. That afternoon I went to the supermarket, and as I got back into the car, someone called my name. Guess who it was? Yes, the same woman I'd thought of that morning, she'd parked right next to me. The other day I was thinking about a lady I knew years ago, wondering if she'd sold her house and where she was living. Two days later, I was on my evening beach walk when a lady cycled up to me and said hi. It was her. She'd bought a house 5 minutes from where I was living. So it's important to acknowledge evidence of when this happens, no matter how insignificant it seems, but simply to see these laws in action. Now, if only I could make that work with Hugh Jackman!

© Creating Healthy Careers 2022

Mind Your Language

An often highly underestimated tool within our power that impacts our ability to turn our beliefs into reality is our language. We can strengthen or create blocks in our careers through language and conversations.

I was coaching a man the other day about his career, and when I asked him what he was good at, he said, "I go into companies that aren't doing well and sort out their shit and fix them up." He saw what he delivered as only being attached to companies that weren't performing well and that he had a battle on his hands to go in and turn them around. It was hard work, and he was exhausted. In seeing things this way, he believed that his lot in life was working with struggling organisations and fixing them up. So, what did he keep attracting throughout his 30-year career? Hard work! We flipped this around to say that he had a talent for helping organisations achieve their potential and be successful, and he found a renewed excitement towards his work. Do you see how that has a different feel to it? We're seeing it through a different lens, one which feels more energising, more at ease, more inspiring. We're removing the negative wording and focusing on the positive. Remember Dr Emoto's rice experiment and the impact different words had on the rice (mentioned in the Introduction)! What can then happen is that changing someone's perspective in one area of their life will have a flow-on effect throughout other areas of their life as well.

Typically you will find if some blocks or patterns are showing up in your career, they're probably happening in other areas of your life as well, and if you correct it in one place, it fixes it in all areas. That's why, when I coach people, they often remark that it's more like life coaching than career coaching. It's all interrelated. Your brain doesn't switch off one set of beliefs when you're thinking about an area of your life and then tap into your work beliefs when you think about work. We're just one giant filing cabinet of beliefs, and if we keep dragging files out from the cabinet, it keeps bringing the past into our future. So if you want to create a new future in your career, stop and look for the patterns that will lead you to a limiting belief running the show, which you can now tackle by following the process in this book.

Notes:

Notes:

CHAPTER 4

CREATING:
Clarity & Alignment

You cannot be
What you cannot see

[MARIAN WRIGHT EDELMAN]

Imagine that before you came into this world, you set intentions of what you were going to do here, what you would achieve and learn, and what experiences you would have to help you grow. However, you lost that clarity of what you intended for your life somewhere along the way. We are never alone though, and Spirit is always there watching over us, trying to guide us by bringing little clues into our life, setting up soul encounters, fated meetings, soul whispers to guide us on our path. We just need to pay attention to when synchronicity is occurring in our life.

In this chapter, I'll take you through a few practical processes that have helped me see the clues life can show us, and I will bring it all together for you so you can start to align your career with your soul purpose.

Now let's take some time to see how it all comes together, and that's precisely where we're going to start, with time.

Create Space

Ever notice how everyone is so busy all the time? When you bump into someone you know and ask, "how are you?" the typical response is "Busy". I was at a girlfriend's for dinner a few months ago with a group of women known to my friend through various business connections. Listening to the conversations around the table, one lady was describing that in addition to being a CEO, she was also on a Board and was about to join another Board and was involved in several other projects and ventures, as if it was a badge of honour to be so busy. This was typical of the conversations around the table. I just sat and observed, and noticed how something didn't feel right within me. All I could think of was how could they be successful and fulfilled at anything when their energy and focus was split across so many activities at once?

This will sound counterintuitive to the people who believe "you have to work hard to be successful" which has been drummed into us throughout most of our lives. The no pain no gain mentality. But how many people do you know who work hard and are not successful, or as successful as they'd like to be? I would guess that is the majority of the population. So why don't we question it and ask ourselves is there a better way? I played that game for many years, but suddenly, that theory started to cause a reaction in me, and when I read Gary Keller's book 'The One Thing', it confirmed my hunch was correct. He talks about choosing your one thing, the main game, and then focusing on that priority.

If you're wondering what this has to do with getting career clarity, stick with me a bit longer.

For the first three years in my business, I'd been splitting my focus in many different directions, doing a range of things, trying to identify my core business, even though I felt I was pretty clear on my purpose. During two of these years, I'd also been a career coach on a program to help people who were 50+ to gain employment. It was gratifying work; however, when that came to an end, I felt a sense of excitement, I could finally create space in my business so I could think. Think about what I wanted to be doing, think about how I could help more people, think about how I could organise all of the tools and knowledge I'd developed over my 30 years in the careers space into a way that could help people. I was ready to distil my knowledge into an online program to reach far more people than I could on a 1:1 basis and really affect the degree of change I'd seen myself doing. I've always had an inner feeling that I want to have a big impact while I'm here, shake things up and get people thinking differently about their careers, and the more I walk my path, the stronger that feeling becomes.

Around this time, I attended an intuitive healing course in the Dandenongs. On the last day, I stood on the balcony, overlooking the beautiful trees and mist drifting across the mountains, and was conversing with the facilitator about, you guessed it, his career path. He'd been working in the engineering space earlier in his career but didn't feel like it was the right path for him any longer, so he decided to take 12 months off and just follow his guidance. During that time, he developed his intuition and created a healing program incorporating a range of modalities including Ayurvedic medicine, Shamanic healing and Psychosomatic principles. This conversation inspired a spark within me, and I decided to do something similar. I was in the process of buying a house, and this was going to enable me to reduce my living expenses, and I'd timed my purchase perfectly to also qualify for a building grant that was available at the time, which put some money back in my pocket! I'd been looking for a house for six months on and off, and on this one particular day, I decided I needed to find something, today, otherwise time would run out. So I drove to six properties that my buyers advocate had identified, selected one, and managed to sign the contract on the last day to qualify for the buyers grant. So now, I'd created the space and some financial backing to enable me to take a step back from life, to strip away all the busyness in my life and take another bold step. I gave myself six months to peel away all of the distractions and focus on my one thing, building and promoting my online program. I gave myself permission to take time and make space in my life, and I was interested to observe what would happen.

At first, it felt strange to have all this time, and I would think to myself, "okay, what do I need to do? Oh, that's right, nothing. " Then I realised it wasn't about doing nothing; it was about clearing my mind and being consciously aware of, and acting on, my guidance. The Chinese have a beautiful proverb, Wu Wei, which means effortless action, or conscious inaction. Just as a river flows around a rock without hesitation or resistance, without trying to fight the rock. Without realising it, I was living the Wu Wei way! I was living consciously in the moment and going with life.

It was about creating quiet so that new thoughts could enter. It was about saying no to things, events and people that didn't align with my 'one thing', or would detract from it. It was about taking action that put me into a feelgood state, like walking and swimming down the beach, journaling, reading, spending time doing what was vital for achieving my 'one thing'. I felt like life was going in slow motion, yet at the same time, I also seemed to be getting a lot done. Christmas arrived, and I didn't even feel like I needed a break, but I took one.

For someone who was taking a step away from work, it was interesting to see how business would come in just when I needed a little financial boost. I learnt to trust that the Universe had my back and let go of trying to make things happen. I was also attracting the next level of clients that I had consciously identified I wanted to work with. I'd started to step up and coach CEO's, Global Divisional Heads and business owners with exciting and challenging problems. I realised that I attracted clients who made me step up my game and develop and implement new tools and knowledge that I'd been drawn to study.

It was not only benefiting me, but it was benefiting my clients. When I was with them, I was refreshed and had the energy to focus on them and new knowledge to share. My mind was clear, the right thoughts and words would come to me in sessions, and I could tune into what was going on for that person. I started to notice that I could also see what was happening behind their words and what was playing out in their lives. I wasn't distracted, rushing to move on to the next client. I was present.

During this time I also clarified what support I needed in my business and finally found the right business/marketing coach (who I'd been looking for over several years). They helped me set up the e-commerce functionality on my website, ensure my messaging spoke to the people I wanted to help, and convey the practical and spiritual elements of the work I do. The bonus, I brought on board a University Marketing Masters intern to help me with marketing research and analytics to improve the marketing of my products and services. So although my one thing was to set up the e-commerce side of my business, not only did I achieve that, I honed my coaching services and attracted the right people to help me. The main goal was the main agenda item each day, and the other things fell in around it if I deemed them essential. It's interesting when you tackle your main goals first, then some of the other smaller distractions seem to fade into the background.

I also had a job offer during this time, however because I was so clear on where I was heading and what I wanted to create, I could graciously decline, knowing that it was in my, and the organisations, best interests.
My message here is that we need to make space in life every now and again to allow new thoughts, ideas and support to enter. There is no room for new information when our mind is full, so we need to create space. Once you decide what you want to achieve and commit to it, the right people, places, and events show up!

Now, not everyone will want to choose the path I took or feel like they can create space in their life due to family or other commitments, and that's okay. My message is to make time for the important things and prioritise them each day. Ask yourself, "what's one thing I can do today to help me get closer to living my career purpose?" and do it – first!

Now, rather than just leave you hanging here to figure out how to gain your career clarity and align your career, I'm going to share some of the tools and techniques I've adapted and created to help me find my career purpose and that many of my clients have found hugely successful in helping them get on their path.

1. *Clarity*

You've already identified some clues of how your life has shaped you through the Join The Dots exercise and by identifying the lessons in the challenges you've experienced throughout your life to see what gifts, talents and experiences your soul journey has equipped you with.

Now we are going to add another final layer to see what's truly important to you by identifying your core values, and then bring it all together to show you what ultimately gives you your reason for being.

The Role Values Play In Your Career Purpose

Knowing and aligning your career with your values is essential, not only in terms of your performance and success, it is also critical to your fulfilment and wellbeing. Values are a guide to indicate whether you are doing what's intrinsically important to you. When we are in a career that enables us to live our highest values, it unlocks passion and drive that sees us pushing through challenges to achieve what we want. The opposite is also true; when we are in a career where we are not living our highest values, or even worse, where our career is in the way of us living our values, we can self-sabotage our performance. Not consciously, as our values are stored in the subconscious mind, and when we're not in alignment, once again, our subconscious tries to come to our rescue and cries, "this isn't the right job for you. This isn't what you love. Let's get you out of here!" Suppose we ignore these messages over many years. In that case, this can ultimately lead to health conditions by harbouring feelings of resentment and frustration without really knowing why, and feeling that life is a constant struggle. I will show in the values ladder shortly the impact living our values has on our careers, success, health, and relationships, but first, let's look at what type of values I am talking about.

Your Voids Become Your Values

Ever wonder why certain things are important to you and not those around you? Why you are passionate about certain causes? How two siblings can grow up in the same household, attend the same school, have the same external influences, and yet have different skills, beliefs and interests? Why do you jump at an opportunity to do something creative at work, and another person gets excited about getting processes and structure in place? What inspires someone to follow a career in the law and another, teaching, and how do you know which path is right for you?

Typically your voids early in your life guide your values. In other words, things that may have been missing in your life when you were a child become important to you, i.e. those misunderstood as a child often become psychologists or counsellors as they help others feel understood. Those who saw injustice in their childhood will often join the police force or become lawyers.

Identifying my values was one of the most powerful processes that had me take action and start my business after seven years of procrastination. The minute I identified my top 3 values (careers, growth and health), I immediately saw what I needed to focus on in my business. I was excited because when I reflected on my life's journey and influences, it was congruent with who I am, what life had shown me and where it had led me. I took action straight away, came up with the business name on the spot, Creating Healthy Careers, and that night I registered the domain and business name. Six months later, I resigned from my full-time job and started my business – after seven years of procrastination. That's how powerful getting clear on your values can be.

I've coached so many people who have plateaued in their careers and didn't know why or what to do about it. They'd lost their career mojo or spark. But once we'd identified their top values and then looked at whether their career was on the way or in the way to living their values, they could see where the misalignment was. We then looked at whether their current employment could be modified to align with their values, if there was another path they could take within their existing organisation, or if they needed to change jobs entirely.

Another area where values can be beneficial is when you're fortunate enough to have two job offers and don't know which one to take. One lady I coached was a single mum, and she had an opportunity to do more or less the same job at higher pay or to pursue her dream job in real estate, with a slight drop in income. Many people in this position may well have been tempted to take the job that offers an immediate higher income; however, after coaching, she understood that staying in the same career would negatively impact her overall fulfilment in life, leaving her feeling disappointed and that this would ultimately have a flow on effect in her life. Plus, she was already on the brink of resenting her career. She decided to back herself, so she chose to follow her dream and only needed to make some life choices in the short term until her salary started to climb. She looked for cheaper accommodation, and as her new role was in a different location where the real estate prices were lower, she had the double bonus of moving closer to work and saving money on rent. It didn't take her long until her salary had returned to a higher level, because when we do what we love, we ultimately do a better job, are giving higher value, and therefore receive higher value for what we do.

It all comes down to choices. Sometimes people know what they want to do and are unhappy in their current career path but don't change. They feel locked in by the 'golden handcuffs' and the need to earn a certain amount of money to fund the lifestyle they want (this is a choice). However, this can be short term thinking and detrimental in the long run. You see, if you stay in a job you hate, it's going to take a toll on your health in the long run, and what does that cost you? When you see the values ladder and how your problem-solving skills, focus and attention to detail open up, you ultimately perform better, and when you perform better, you earn better – you're valued and achieve your value.

How To Identify Your Values

If you look around, many people are talking about the importance of values and the various methods to help you draw out your values. It can be very confusing. Many organisations have values on their websites; however, these are typically words like "respect, integrity, honesty". These are not the values I'm talking about. They are values to hold your performance accountable to, but these values aren't going to get you jumping out of bed with excitement to face your day or make you find the inspiration to keep going when times get tough. So we need to see what your subconscious mind prioritises as vital to you. What's going to have you take action and give you some clarity around what you need to have present in your career to achieve success, in all meanings of the word.

The values work I undertook in Michael's three day seminar centres around the work of Dr John Demartini, who has a passion for learning and teaching people how values impact their life and health and what drives the unconscious mind when it comes to decision-making and prioritizing things in our lives. The following values ladder will show you what happens when you are in a career aligned with your top values and also when your job isn't aligned. See what rings true for you.

Values Ladder
When you live your highest values you'll be inspired and inspiring!

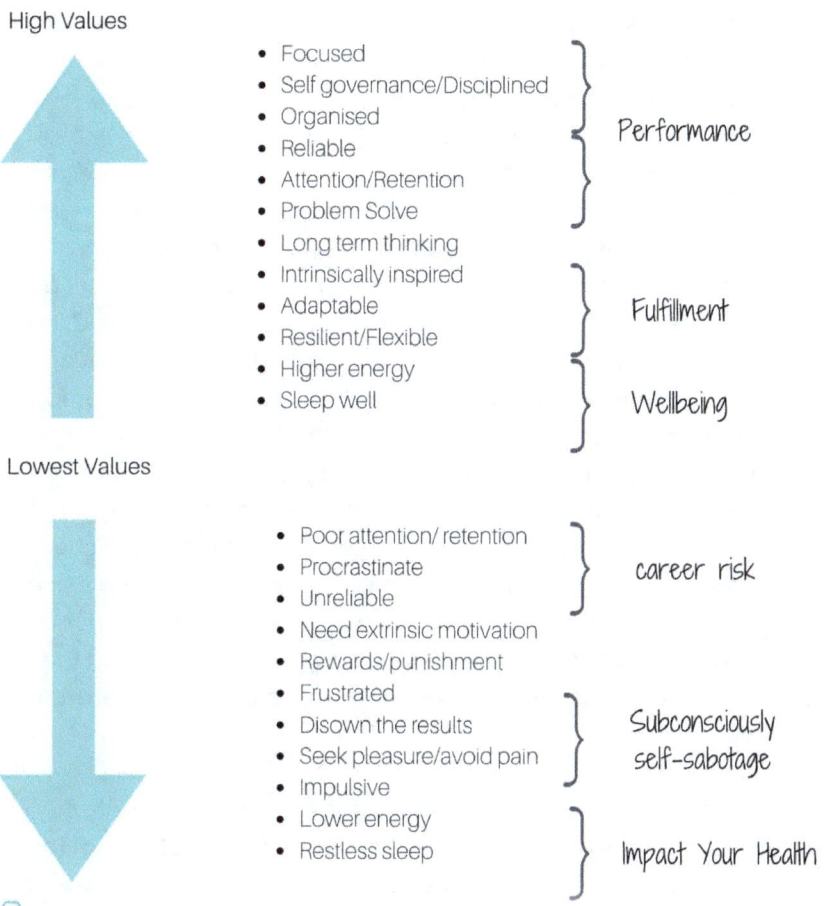

Based On Dr John Demartini's Values Ladder

I've added the last two bullet points around energy and sleep to the ladder because that's what I've observed as common symptoms having coached people over the years. This demonstrates the link between values and wellbeing.

I mentioned before that when your values are not aligned with your career, interestingly you can subconsciously self-sabotage your performance because you're not doing something you love. Or sometimes external circumstances (usually in the form of an unpleasant challenge) can arise to force our hand if we are not proactively taking action towards alignment. I quite often remind people of this when they've identified they want to move on and then start to hesitate and say, "perhaps it's not too bad here after all; perhaps I should stay?". Remember my story, I kept procrastinating and going from job to job rather than starting my business, and during that time, experienced several wake-up calls? Just yesterday, I was coaching a lady who had taken redundancy and was eager to be working again. A friend suggested a job, but it was not in an area of interest to her. She wondered if she should entertain it or not and if she was being too fussy. This is when you come back to check if a job will enable you to live your values or not. The risk was if she went into a job just for the sake of it, in due course, her performance would decline because her heart wouldn't be in it, which would then impact her self-confidence gradually being eroded. So there are many flow-on effects to consider.

Another 'sciency' fact, from a neuroscience perspective, is that when you are doing a task you enjoy, more blood flows to that part of the brain, so neural connections are formed faster, which increases problem-solving and creative abilities. Therefore you perform better. I'm laughing to myself because five years ago when I sat in on that three day personal development course and Michael was speaking about a whole lot of science stuff, I wondered, "what the heck has this got to do with anything." Now, I love it!

So how do you identify your values? You can go onto Dr John Demartini's website and undertake his values determination assessment for free. It will produce a graph for you, clearly showing how you prioritise your values, and will give you some important questions to consider (drdemartini.com./values). I have also presented an abbreviated version of this process to get you to start thinking about what's important to you below.

Step 1: Identifying What's Important

Ask yourself these questions and write down three responses that come to mind for each:

What do you enjoy doing in your spare time?

....

....

....

What do you spend most of your time thinking & talking about?

....

....

....

....

What do you choose to spend your money on?

....

....

....

....

What do you dream/fantasise about doing or having in your life?

....

....

....

....

If I was to walk around your home, what would I notice about you?

....

....

....

....

What do you like to read about or research, or watch online?

....

....

....

....

What goals have you consistently focused on in your life?

....

....

....

....

In which areas of your life are you most organised?

....

....

....

....

What activities energise you?

....

....

....

....

What activities do you 'get lost in' (in the zone)?

....

....

....

....

What makes your heart happy/makes you the most fulfilled in life?

....

....

....

....

What Apps are you constantly looking at and why?

....

....

....

....

What inspires you?

....

....

....

....

What do you consistently prioritise in your life?

....

....

....

....

....

....

Step 2: Categorise

Group similar answers together and then come up with a name for that category*. Some suggested categories might be: health, wealth creation, security, creativity, learning, achievement, contribution, meaning & purpose, joy, teaching, growth, experiences, sports, wellbeing, family, spirituality, fitness, travel, connection, community, nature, knowledge, food, helping others, variety, adventure, animals, sustainability, the environment.

List similar interests together.	Give your Category a Name

*When you are coming up with a name for each category, stop and ask, "What do these things mean to me, or what does it bring into my life?" For example, I was coaching a person one day, and they came back with one of their top values as their dogs.

When I asked them what their dogs meant to them, they said they were their family. So the value was family. Another area you may need to dig a bit deeper into is money. It may be valid that wealth creation is in itself a top value of yours, but also ask what money means to you. Is it more about the adventures it will provide, the security, or are you fascinated and inspired to grow wealth? I was running a workshop, and one of the participants was embarrassed that money had come up as one of his top values. He felt that he 'should' have values that reflected something more meaningful. When I told him that Warren Buffet, one of the richest men in the world, has wealth creation as one of his top values and that it's perfectly fine to be inspired by that, he felt relieved. So whenever you hear yourself saying 'should,' that is usually a sign that you are subordinating what's important to you to what's important to others so that others won't judge you.

Step 3: Prioritise

NOW LIST THE SEVEN CATEGORIES YOU HAVE NAMED:

1.
2.
3.
4.
5.
6.
7.

> *(You can add up how many answers you had for each category in the above table and prioritise and see if that rings true for you, or you may have a sense as you compare one value with another, which one is more important).*

Now ask yourself, "Is my career aligned with my top values?" and "does my career allow me to live my top values?" and pay attention to your gut reaction here. Any 'aha' moments here for you? Suppose you've been in a slump in your career and focused on the negative aspects of your job. In that case, this exercise might help you realise that the career or job you're in ticks the most important boxes for you, and you've simply been focusing on the 10% that you don't enjoy. This exercise can reconnect you with why you do what you do and reinvigorate your interest. Or, it might help you reconnect with the fact that family and adventure are your top values. Then you link all the ways your career benefits your family and how it enables you to have adventures, moving your career up the list in your subconscious mind. And just on family, if that is one of your top values, I encourage you to dig deeper and ask yourself what family means to you. It will help to identify specific characteristics, such as love, belonging, connection or support, which you can then seek within your career as well.

However, another result of this exercise is that it clarifies what's missing from your career and can point to why you're not happy, helping you realise what you want in your job. We are all influenced early on in life by the opinions of others – our family, our teachers, our friends. Everyone can tend to have a say on what we 'should' do in our career, and we can end up following a path because it's what everyone else wanted for us or thought would be good for us. I've seen many people reach their 40's or even 50's and say, "I've been doing this all my life, but I don't know why and I don't enjoy it, but I don't know what I want to do." It can take courage to pivot your career later in life, but it's worth it. I was coaching a lady who was in her early 60's, and she was contemplating a career change, but it required her to undertake some further study. She asked, "should I not bother and just see out my years doing the same work I'm doing now?" You can imagine my thoughts, especially because her job was negatively impacting her health, but as the conversation continued, she admitted that she wanted to be doing something worthwhile for the rest of her life and enjoying it, so she had her answer!

We can also dig deeper to identify your specific career values.

Think of a time you were happiest in your career and ask yourself what was present, to elicit your values. Values are commonly one word. If you come up with a sentence, ask yourself, why is that important to me?

Then quickly number the top 5 that stand out for you.

2. *Alignment*

This is where we bring it all together to see how you can align your skills, strengths, gifts, talents with your career purpose.

One tool I have adapted for my career coaching business that helps translate all of the insights you've uncovered so far into a career that aligns with your purpose is the Ikigai model. The Ikigai model has been used to show why the Japanese have such longevity in life. Japan is classified as one of the blue zones around the world where people live a long and healthy life and are still active contributors in their communities. This model shows what gives them meaning, purpose, and a sense of contribution which, apart from diet, are the significant factors that contribute to a long and healthy life.

So I'll take you through how to convert this model into four key career questions that will help you identify your Career Sweet Spot and help you steer your career onto the path you're seeking.

Creating

Ikigai
A JAPANES CONCEPT MEANING "A REASON FOR BEING"

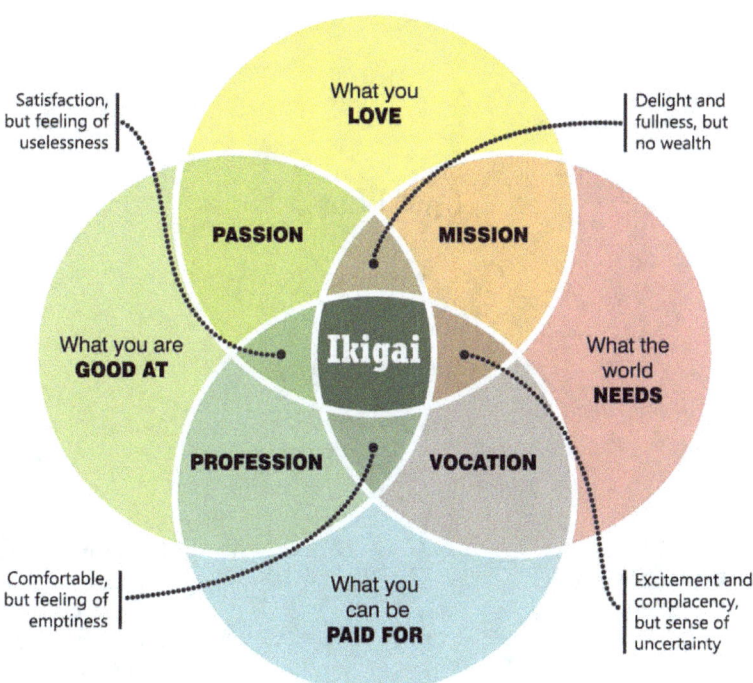

This diagram shows that it is essential to have four key elements present to achieve a 'Reason for Being', and these are the four critical areas for you to look at to see how you can gain a sense of meaning and purpose in your career.

1. Doing what you are good at (using your strengths, gifts, talents)
2. Doing something you love (that you're passionate about, brings you joy or something that is in line with your top values)
3. Doing something the world needs (how you contribute, what

85

problems do you solve, where you add value) (we'll touch on your value proposition in the next chapter)

4. Taking 1, 2 and 3 above into account, what career paths does that lead to, where will you be valued?

Or in summary:

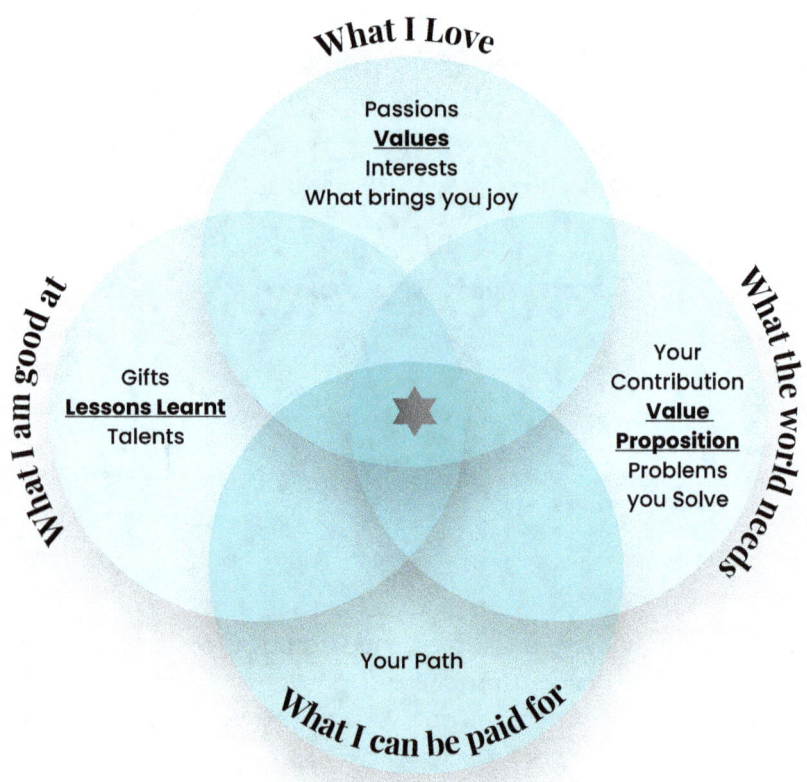

The way to put this into practice is to ask yourself these four questions and start to list everything you think of. It's important to be open-minded and not censor your answers because you never know how it might all link up and what thoughts it might provoke. I have noticed that people might have ideas that lead to another idea they wouldn't have thought about if they had stopped themselves. So approach it with an open mind and write down whatever comes to mind. We want to keep writing and see what comes up.

At the end of this exercise, you will have many thoughts floating around in your head; however, when it comes to finding alignment with our career purpose, we also want to think with our hearts. One way I learnt to tune into my heart was through a friend of mine who is a Heart Healer, Susie Dolling. Her technique is to tune into your heart by putting your left hand on your heart, closing your eyes, taking three deep breaths, and then asking yourself a question, like: 'what do I really want to do?' or whatever question you would like an answer to. Then wait and listen to what pops into your head. Don't dismiss the first thought as being a mistake. This is your heart talking to you and it speaks softly.

Another way to start to gain an insight into your career purpose is to ask yourself each day, what gave you inspiration and meaning the day before? The clues are always there in front of us, we just need to take the time to pay attention.

Exploration

I spoke earlier in this chapter about giving yourself space and time, and it's important to touch on it again here.

You might find that once you've completed the Ikigai model, you have a list that doesn't give you clear answers. If that's the case, then you are likely in what I call The Exploration Phase, and that's perfectly fine. It's an important step we need to permit ourselves to take. This is a critical stage in the self-discovery process and one that we don't usually allow ourselves any time to pursue. I have noticed that when people have decided they want a career change, they want to get from A to B as soon as possible and don't factor in any time to explore what they want to be doing in their next job. It's such a critical stage because if they don't stop and explore what they want and what might be possible, they will jump at anything simply to get out of their current situation. As a career coach, I find that part of my job is to give people permission to spend some time in this exploration phase because they often felt like they needed to have it all worked out straight away.

It's all very well to explore, but what does that look like? What does that involve? Even having worked in recruitment for over 25 years, I knew a lot of organisations and what they did, and what type of jobs existed, but I didn't have all the answers. So how do you get the answers?

You might start by tapping into your network, friends, family, people you know who work in a particular industry you're interested in. Go and speak with them and see what ideas they might have. Everyone in your network could be of assistance because they might know someone or something that you don't, and they can refer you to pursue a particular path of enquiry.

Another way is to spend some time putting yourself in new environments to see what lights you up. You might have a skill set that you've suppressed for so long you've forgotten about it, and by taking up a hobby, all of a sudden, you are reminded of your passion for creativity, for example. A friend of mine has buried her passion for design while she's worked in the corporate sector, and is currently designing, building and furnishing her forever home. It's made her passion come to life. She has a real flare for it, and I'm keen to see if this opportunity might spark a career change into interior design, which she would love. The seed has been planted!

Have a look back at what you've written under the heading "What I Love" in the Ikigai model and see what industries come to mind. Then make a list of what organisations fit into those industries and contact those companies to see what jobs your skillsets would fit into.

I can remember hearing a Ted Talk by a lady who'd taken a year off to try out different jobs to get an idea of what she enjoyed (they were all casual or contract roles). When she stepped into one she'd dreamed about (I think it was working on a farm because of her love for animals and the outdoors), she recognised it didn't match what she'd imagined. So if you can create some space in your life to take that approach, give it a go! In reality, this might be a luxury that many of us can't make work in our lives, so an alternative could be to perhaps look at things like volunteering or going part-time in your current role to try another position on a part-time basis, or do some contracting work for a while to try out different jobs.

Notes:

Notes:

---- CHAPTER 5 ----

EMERGENCE:
Stepping Into the Person You Are Here To Become

You find your path
On your path

[YOURS TRULY]

Don't you think you've been hiding your true self away for long enough? It's time to step into the person you are here to be! What are you waiting for? Courage?

Let me tell you the truth about courage. We think we need to wait until we've got courage before we do something, but the truth is, it's in taking action that we get the courage. I've taken plenty of leaps of faith, and I've never felt courageous in the process, so does courage actually exist? Either way, don't wait until you feel 'bulletproof' before you take a step on your path; otherwise, you could be waiting a lifetime. Accept that fear and uncertainty may still be present, but acknowledge yourself for stepping out of your comfort zone to make something amazing happen in your life.

When I first learnt Theta Healing, I wondered, "how am I going to do this with people who haven't experienced theta healing before? They'll think I'm weird!". You see, the actual process of downloading new beliefs requires the practitioner to go into a theta state, so you are sitting in front of your client with your eyes closed, observing what's going on and not talking. I can remember being in a session for the first time after I completed my training, and the need came up to use theta healing. The voice in my head was telling me "just to do it", but I was fighting with myself because I thought I'd be judged and appear unprofessional (years of conditioning working in the corporate world). I knew it was effective, and I love modalities that are a bit different, but I hadn't embraced my 'weird & wonderful' yet.

I took a breath and told the client what I was going to do, and it was a fabulous experience. She had been holding herself back in her career and wanted to step into coaching as a career. When I went into a theta state, I saw her with chains pinning her down and a brick wall in front of her blocking her from moving forward. Then she became a warrior woman, knocked the wall down, and broke the chains. There were also two stars shining above her. When I relayed what I'd seen during the session, she was moved. The warrior woman meant something special to her. She also interpreted the two stars to be the souls of the two babies she'd miscarried and saw them as looking out for her. She came to life. The fear left her, and she felt supported to move forward in her life. So if I hadn't dared to be myself, she wouldn't have experienced the same outcome from our session.

It took me a while to break the corporate mold I'd created for myself over 30 years and step into the real me, a blend of the practical, spiritual, and intuitive. I acknowledged that I'd received skills, wisdom and experiences (as we all have) so that I could help others, and so who was I to say "no thank you, I'm not doing that" and run the risk of clients not benefiting, and me not living my true soul purpose. I can imagine what would have happened if I'd rejected my path. Now, think about yourself. What direction are you turning away from, what skills, gifts and talents are you hiding from the world? Who are you to get in the way of what you are here to do? Think of all of those people that may miss out on your help, or the joy you might bring into their world, if you get in your own way!

In Chapter 3 we looked at clearing any blocks holding you back by identifying and reprogramming your beliefs, so now you're free to emerge as the new you. Part of that process involved recognising your gifts and talents and what you are here to do. You would have already started to get a strong sense of this from Chapters 2 and 4, but let's take a deeper look into how you are here to contribute, and how to identify your true value proposition.

Becoming the Person You're Here To Be

We've already gone through several exercises in Chapters 2 and 4 to help you identify your gifts (Join the Dots, your values and Ikigai), and you've looked at life events that have shaped you to see what skills and knowledge they have equipped you with. Here we were looking for the clues in your past to help shape your future. Now we are going to look back into your past to find the skills, gifts and talents that are congruent with the future you are moving into, and who you are here to be.

I'm going to give you a different spin on the Join the Dots exercise that you did in Chapter 4. In that chapter, I mentioned the Steve Jobs quote that you can't join the dots looking forward; you can only join the dots looking back. I want to offer you another lens through which to view your 'dots' when you are looking to create a new path in your career, and might be lacking the self-belief to make it happen.

This concept came up in a conversation during a liquid crystals session I had with John Mather, an Advanced Liquid Crystal Practitioner in Adelaide. Liquid crystals are a fascinating modality designed to bring awareness to what characteristics you were born into, then identify where you're operating from your shadow self, and bring you back to your authentic self by ingesting the properties of various liquid crystal drops. However, it was in the conversation I had with John that I realised there was another way to use the Join the Dots exercise to create a new future.

When you initially did the Join The Dots exercise, you identified significant life events, influencers, and influences from your past, looking for the lessons in those events/encounters, what they equipped you with, and how they shaped your career path. We were looking for clues in your past to make sense of your present.

What I discovered in my session with John is that when we have a vision of something we want to create in our future, we can identify what characteristics are needed to become the type of person to achieve that vision, and then look for the dots in our past, our foundations, that line up with that vision. This gives us evidence that we already have what we need to step into that version of us, or bring those characteristics to life. We start with a vision of what we'd like to do, and go back in our past, to our foundations, and find clues that validate that career vision.

You've done enough work in earlier chapters to have a sense of clarity around what your career purpose is, so now I want you to dream big. Be honest with yourself. What is it you'd love to do? Now ask yourself, what characteristics, experience, wisdom would it take to do that? Who do I need to become? Then I want you to have a look back in your past for evidence of these characteristics, experiences and knowledge in your 'foundations'. For example, my vision for the second phase of my business is to work with CEO's to help them re-establish organisational purpose and for their renewed inspiration to be infectious throughout the organisation and ultimately the people they are here to serve. Before moving forward in my business, I need to see myself as a match for these clients, an equal, not necessarily having experienced everything they have, but having a foundation of skills, characteristics and wisdom that will be of benefit to these clients. The characteristics that come to mind are risk-taking, resilience, the ability to stay true to what they value in the face of judgement, go against the norm if needed and take action in the face of fear. When I looked at it that way, I could see evidence of possessing these traits in my past which then gave me more confidence that I'm up to the challenge.

A couple of months after this, I started attracting clients that were consistent with my new vision: a CEO, a Global Marketing Director and a Human Resources Director, and I'm excited to see what comes my way next!

This example demonstrates that your purpose needs to be landed within you before you can attract it. You attract who you are, so you need to shift yourself and your perspective of who you are into that person you want to become. Recognise that you already have what you need in your foundation. However, there is one proviso, you need to address what you've attracted and created until now to move away from it. Chapter 3 will help you release those past beliefs and programs created from your childhood that are still shaping who you are and what you are attracting today. Discovering my purpose and getting on my path had been part of my initial personal journey and they say you teach what you learn, so in the first phase of my business, I helped people do the same. So you need to become aware of where you are birthing the new you from. If you're still holding onto old programs and beliefs, that's what you'll continue to attract. I had been attracting clients and work congruent with my lessons from childhood, so I needed to keep digging and clearing to make space for something new.

How To Embody Your Gifts

This is where you start to get to know your path a little further. Often people have an awakening later in their career as they look back and think, "I've been doing the same thing for so long, but I'm no longer getting the same level of fulfilment out of it", and they start to feel like they've drifted off track in life. This is a big topic to explore, and we often feel a lot of pressure from society to know our purpose or our 'Why'. However if you approach it from a place of desperation, thinking you're not complete until you've got this missing piece of the puzzle, you're going to hold yourself in the space of resistance and pressure, and that's not going to open up the creative thinking part of your brain, the neocortex, which is the area that will send answers your way. Instead, the blood will flow to the amygdala, which runs the fight/flight/freeze response, and this is when you end up with brain fog. So we want to create a space of enquiry to open up your mind, and as I often say to clients, it's not a case of completing a questionnaire and waiting for the computer to spit out the answers. You have the answers. We just need to focus on the right questions and draw them out. So this is something that only you can do. A coach will help guide some of the conversations, but you can do this independently.

A warning here: this can also be one of those processes that people can spend a lifetime dwelling on and end up not taking any action – analysis paralysis. I've seen people get stopped in their tracks by assuming they have to have it all worked out before taking the first step. The reality is that sometimes action precedes clarity. In other words, it's in taking the first step that the clarity comes. Ever heard the expression "jump, and build the plane on the way down"? Now I'm not saying just leap, and the inspired thoughts will come to you on the way. They will, but you do want to start with some vision, purpose or direction in mind, and then as you take some steps, further clarity will unfold.

I'm here to help you get some answers now to gain clarity and inspiration in your career and have you take action now. If you wait to have clarity before you take action, you'll be waiting a long time before you start moving in that direction. So the message for you here is not to be impatient and not to seek perfection, but make a start and now you've learnt how to observe the clues in life, keep an eye open along the way so you can keep gaining clarity.

Remember I spoke earlier about the Exploration Phase? If you overlook this critical stage, you'll put immense pressure on yourself to come up with the answer and to make a change right now. So be kind to yourself. Spend time being curious and paying attention to what causes a positive reaction in you. In this case, close enough is good enough, so once you have a sense that you are in the neighbourhood of your purpose, start walking in that direction, and you will find your path on your path. When I began, I thought I had a rock-solid intention – helping people to achieve career wellbeing. To get into a career that was good for their health. Four years in, this is still an underpinning theme, however it looks somewhat different from when I started, as reflected in this book!

I was catching up with a lady a while ago who had been diagnosed with cancer many years earlier, and she told me the day she received her diagnosis, she meditated. She experienced deep bliss and, in that process, suddenly became aware of how much she wanted to live. She then started receiving visions of her life's purpose. She continued to receive other pieces of the puzzle as the years go by and she said that she's realised that our purpose unfolds during our lifetime, we don't necessarily have an epiphany and see the ultimate vision all at once.

I feel that we want our lives to have a purpose, and we can start to identify what that is for us now, but don't feel that once you have written it down, you are wed to that path and no other for the rest of your life. We start down a path, and then another path may open up. It will evolve, and the Universe will reveal what you are ready for when the time is right. Dolores Cannon, a well known hypnotherapist who used to receive spiritual guidance through her clients in session, used to say that her guidance was constantly drip-fed to her and that when she asked why, it was explained that it's similar to a baby's development. First, they start accepting milk, then soft foods, the solids. If you introduce solids too early, the baby won't be ready and won't be able to handle it. It's the same with us when it comes to our purpose.

So, where to start?

We've talked before about how the answers are within you. We've also talked about the power of the mind. So start to ask your mind to reveal to you what your purpose is. A great time to do this is when you are going to bed and drifting off to sleep, and ask your mind, your guide, infinite intelligence (whatever sits comfortably with you) to show you signs of what your purpose is. You might have dreams that give you some clues once your conscious mind is out of the way. Give it a try and see what happens. Don't give up after one night. Keep trying it. Sometimes the subconscious mind doesn't reveal things to our conscious mind until we are ready. Perhaps keep a notepad next to your bed. You can also ask this question once you are in a meditative state. This is where the heart healing method can also help, where you put your left hand on your heart, take three deep breaths, ask the question out loud and then wait and see what messages enter your mind.

Now it's over to you to spend some valuable time asking yourself these questions and self-reflecting. Have fun discovering what's under the surface that you've probably always known, but now, are bringing it into vision.

What would you love to do?

....
....
....
....

What would you love to be remembered for when you are no longer here?

....
....
....
....

Future pace your life. Stop and think; you are now 80 years old. You've taken the safe, comfortable road and not taken the risk you wanted to. What's your biggest regret? The thing you always wanted to do but never did?

....
....
....
....

Think of a day at work when, as you headed home, you might have said to yourself, "I would have done that for free!" What happened to make you say that?

....

....

....

....

....

Then, keep writing .....

My purpose is ....

....

My purpose is ....

....

My purpose is ....

....

I've watched clients do this exercise, and the power is in just starting to write, and then each time you write, new words and thoughts will come to mind.

Your Secret Weapon — Your Value Proposition

One critical lesson I've learnt in my career is that it's more important to recognise my value than rely on external validation of my value and worth.

There was a time when I didn't feel valued by the person I was reporting to, and the benefit of this wake-up call was that I took a close look at what truly gave me a feeling of being valued. It wasn't a pat on the back. It was the difference I was making to the people I was helping. At that moment, everything changed, and I started to value myself more. This was the final piece of the puzzle I needed before I stepped out and started my business.

Understanding your value proposition will give you a feeling of empowerment and increase your confidence. It also helps you see how your gifts and talents are here to help others. Posing this question to candidates about their value proposition would stop most people in their tracks. We don't think of ourselves this way, especially in our careers. We typically think about what we want and what we are good at but knowing where and how we add value is essential.

How can we feel valued if we don't know how we add value? As we touched on in Chapter 4 when looking at the Ikigai model, the third circle is about discovering what the world needs and how you contribute. When we see how we are able to contribute to the bigger picture, it gives us a sense of belonging.

One way to identify your value proposition is depicted in this diagram, which shows that when you identify how your skills, gifts and talents contribute to the needs of someone else, you feel valued:

THEM

Their Problems
Their wants & needs
Their values

Return on Investment

VALUE

Meaning and Fulfillment

YOU

Your Skills
Your Values
Your Purpose

Here are some questions to help you identify your overall value proposition:

What do people naturally gravitate towards you for?

What has been your legacy in previous roles?

What lights you up when you are doing it?

What have you been asked to run training sessions on or train others in?

What has given you the most incredible sense of career fulfilment or satisfaction?

....
....
....
....

What do your colleagues, friends or family regularly ask you for advice on?

....
....
....
....

Where have you made the most significant difference/ contribution?

....
....
....
....

What are you sought out for? What are you the 'go to' person for?

....

....

....

....

What type of projects do you get asked to be involved in?

....

....

....

....

If clients have written any testimonials about your service, what do they say?

....

....

....

....

Now review what you've written in the questions above and highlight the keywords that stand out to you.

Now write out:

My value proposition is ....

....

My value proposition is ....

....

My value proposition is ....

....

My value proposition is ....

....

So now you have all the tools to view your gifts, talents and knowledge from a different perspective and understand that when you recognise your value, you will be confident to step into your career purpose.

Notes:

CHAPTER 6

ATTRACTION:
Create It, Feel It, Attract It

*What is right for you
Wants to come to you*

[A COURSE IN MIRACLES]

Before we go through the steps of what it takes to attract your dream career, let's start with a brief understanding of some of the Universal laws that govern attraction.

It Starts With A Thought

At the business breakfast I spoke about in the Introduction, when I uttered, "Sometimes I think I should just sell my house and start my business", I didn't realise then that I was setting the wheels in motion. That was the first step in converting something from the metaphysical (my thoughts and images) into the physical. You see, I'd had a thought which sparked a vision. That vision made me feel excited, and those feelings inspired me to express it in words. I'd made a statement about what I wanted. Then the cycle started. I kept thinking about it, feeling it, writing down my dream and plans, seeing it in my mind, talking to more people about it. Then eventually, mixed with a bit of motivation (lack of money), I put the plan into action. Question for a moment, what are the odds of selling a house in 3 days without advertising it? The plan may have been lying dormant for a few years, but it was always on the radar, waiting to leap into being at the right time. So please don't give up on your vision, your timing might just be off, and trust that the timing is all for your highest good. After all, those extra years working in other jobs expanded my skills, knowledge and self-belief, and gave me further experiences which would prove valuable to help my clients.

Let's take a step back and look at this. If that thought hadn't first arisen, would those moving pieces have all fallen into place in Divine timing, just as my funds were running out? Conditions were forming around me to have me take the action I needed to (to follow my dream and start my business). The conditions had to be just right because otherwise, I might not have reached out to the real estate agent, I might not have sold my house, I might not have taken the plunge and stepped away from my job. It's like the ripple effect that all starts with one thought, but you have to be a willing participant in the process. You need to decide!

Can I ask you, how often do you actually ask yourself what you'd love to do? Do you ever spend time visualising how you want your life to be? Do you ever share those dreams with anyone, express them in words and write them down? Quite often, we'll think about life from the perspective of absence – what's missing in our life, or we'll complain about the things in our career that we're not happy with: a micro-managing boss, a colleague that's giving you grief, a client that's giving us a hard time. Do you ever dream big and think of what you'd like?

I've heard it from a few sources, Delores Cannon being one of them; imagine if your life is a play and you are the writer, director and actor, how would you write it? Well, that's lesson 101 of manifestation when it comes to your career. Get a clear vision of what you want, and hopefully, you are now well on your way to doing that!

To create and attract your dream job, you need to clarify what lights you up. A crucial ingredient in the attraction process is the emotion you feel when you think of what you want. The emotion helps you get on the same energetic frequency as that thing you want. Some of the most powerful emotions are excitement, desire, love, hope and enthusiasm, so we need to dream of a job that generates those emotions within us. Something worth noting here is how important it is to be conscious about who you spend your time with. If you're hanging around people who gossip, or only talk about negative topics, complain about their jobs, or are the glass half empty type, or you just don't feel good around them, then you have a few decisions to make. Managing your mindset should always be your fundamental aim.

Let's start by outlining some of the Universal Laws that are at play. By recognising these, you will better understand how to use them as guiding principles in your life and why visualisation that we spoke of in Chapter 3 is so powerful.

The Laws of Vibration & Attraction

What you attract into your life starts with you.

You may be well aware of these laws, and I might not be sharing anything new here, however, if this is your first look into this world, this is where you will need to allow your mind to go places it hasn't gone before.

Let's start by seeing how energy plays a role in manifestation. Everything is made of energy, including us, and energy operates at various frequencies and attracts other energies operating at the same frequencies. Energy is ubiquitous and moves into form when the observer is present. As we showed in Chapter 3 when I touched on the ground-breaking quantum physics experiment called the double slit experiment (or the observer effect), that showed how waves and particles behave differently and follow form when an observer is present. The fact that someone is adding their powers of observation to the particles makes them behave differently! So we cause energy to take a specific form.

Another way of looking at it was touched on in Dr Joe Dispenza's book "Breaking the Habit of Being You" when he refers to Albert Einstein's famous equation $E = mc2$, showing that energy and matter are fundamentally related and interchangeable, explaining how our thoughts create our reality. "At the subatomic level, energy responds to your mindful attention and becomes matter." So our thoughts cause energy to come into form. We are doing it all the time but mostly without consciously directing our thoughts to what we want. We often focus on the negative, which we attract more of into our lives. "Where attention goes, energy flows."

When it comes to getting on your path, the big challenge many people have is that often people are looking to move into a new job because they are unhappy in their current situation and are therefore operating at a lower vibration. Trust me, I've been there and know how important it is to get yourself in a better feeling state first to attract something at a higher vibration. Plus it's a case of believing it before you see it. Remember, new thoughts create new feelings, which drive actions that deliver different results! You can enact many strategies to change your headspace, and some are identified further down in this chapter.

The Law of Cause & Effect

This law explains that every cause has an effect and every effect has its cause. Think of Newton's Third Law: for every action, there is an equal and opposite reaction. Picture a pendulum, each time the balls collide on one side, they conduct energy that causes the balls on the other side to swing out to the same degree. Every effect you see in your outside world has a cause that started in your inner world, in your mind, with a thought. See how powerful your thoughts are! Your subconscious mind takes each thought that creates a picture in your mind and interprets that as something you want. Then sets about making that a reality in your outside world. It's already at work in your life without you being conscious of it, so why not make this work for you? Start seeing yourself in the job you truly want and spend time each day visualising that picture and feel the feelings as you do.

How Do You Get There From Here?

So how do we make that happen? How do we get ourselves into a higher vibration when we may be dreading going into work each day, spending our time avoiding certain people, conversations or tasks and getting caught up in conversations about how unhappy we are? Let me share a secret with you. The subconscious mind hears everything we say and can't discern whether it is true or false or something we want or don't. It then takes that order and works towards making that wish a reality. You are already manifesting what is happening in your life, whether you know it or not. So now's the time to have some conscious input to create what you want. So why aren't all your dreams coming true? Well, unfortunately we have many conflicting thoughts that go against what we truly want. For example, you might want to have a highly successful business, and picture it, but one again, those hidden beliefs pop up under the surface to tell you you're not worthy.

Here are some suggested strategies to help get you into a space that feels better and change your mindset right now, regardless of how unpleasant your current situation is:

1. Identify something that you enjoy about your job and focus on it, savour it, be grateful for it and try and spend as much time thinking about it, or doing that thing, as possible.

2. Reduce the energy you put into the negative – both through your thoughts and words – mind your language, the conversations you have and the people you spend your time with.

3. Schedule time to worry – rather than carrying negative or worrying thoughts around all day, actually schedule time in your calendar and set 20 minutes aside to worry. After 5 minutes, I guarantee you will be bored. This practice ensures that you are not having constant thoughts all day about the 'bad' parts of your job, and you are only focussing energy on it for a limited time.

4. This one is from Bob Proctor, who ultimately got the idea from Napoleon Hill from 'Think and Grow Rich'. It's using a goal card to trigger the image of what you want so that you only have to touch that card to activate the picture in your mind. This then sets off the emotions which ultimately bring about what you're thinking of.

5. One great way to get out of your head is to focus on helping someone else. It could be a client, a colleague, your manager. Whoever it is, if you focus on helping whomever you come into contact with, it will shift your thoughts onto them, and it has the flow-on effect of making you feel great because you've helped someone. What happens is that positive events will start to flow back to you in the way others treat you – remember Cause & Effect!
6. When your thoughts are spiralling down a negative path, change the path by asking yourself, "What would I love?" This will start you thinking about how you want your life to be, shifting your emotional state.

Create It: Your Dream Job (Description)

You may recall my Wakeup Call #1 in Chapter 1 when my job was at risk, and I wanted to move out of recruitment but didn't know what else I could do. One of the steps I took was to create my dream job description, and within two weeks, that job appeared, and I got it! This is how it happened.

I wrote out a list that looked something like this:

1. Meeting with people and talking about their businesses
2. Finding out what works and what doesn't work
3. How do they solve problems
4. Providing solutions
5. Connecting people
6. Helping people be more successful
7. Understanding what makes people successful in a job
8. Learning how people's careers unfolded
9. Getting out of the office to talk with people
10. Having autonomy over my day
11. Working with interesting, like-minded people

12. Working somewhere where my input is valued
13. Work in the city
14. Setting how much I want to earn
15. To work a nine-day fortnight.

I then started to put all this information down on paper, and it looked like a Job Description. Then I looked at everything I'd written and realised that it fell into the scope of a Business Development role. Although a big part of being a recruitment consultant was winning your work, I hadn't held the position of a Business Development Manager, so I didn't think I'd have a competitive chance of winning this type of role in a completely new industry. As I always say, it's challenging to make two career moves in one move, i.e. job title and industry, so I needed to find a role somehow related to careers. So I started spreading the word amongst my network, and within two weeks, this exact role, a BDM within the careers sector, had appeared on Seek, and one of my contacts also brought it to my attention. A week later, I had the job. It had everything on my list, and more!

So this is a great exercise to help you get clear on what you might want to be doing next and give you the clarity to attract it. What is critical in this process is to feel into the role. Once you've painted a picture of it, spend time seeing yourself in your ideal job and connect with the feelings. Perhaps go to a place near where you want to work, and spend some time in a nearby café pretending you're on your lunch break or waiting for a meeting. The art of visualisation is so critical in bringing your dream into reality.

Another tip to have some fun creating your dream job is to look at various job ads, and when you read something that excites you and aligns with your skills and values, copy and paste that into your dream job description. Why not, we're creating our dream job!

This exercise is vital; articulating what you want and seeing it when the opportunity presents itself. It's like the old story about buying a particular model of car, say a blue SAAB convertible (a previous dream of mine), and once you've decided that you want to get one, all of a sudden you start to see that car everywhere. Is that because more SAAB convertibles are around? No, of course not. It's because they are on your radar (in your RAS), and you are seeing them and noticing them. They move from your unconscious mind to your conscious mind.

Manifesting your dream job isn't just about thinking about it; it's about taking some action too! So start to create your dream job description here:

Your Dream Job Description

Company:
- Values
- Size – small, international – could provide travel opportunities
- Industry
- Benefits (development, perks, flexibility)
- Location
- Provide training and support

People:
- Culture
- Level of professionalism, relaxed work environment
- Management/leadership style
- Co-workers

Role Requirements:
- Degree of autonomy
- Report to a mentor or industry expert you can learn from
- Salary, bonus
- Opportunity for growth

Responsibilities:
- What do I enjoy doing and would be happy to do 80% of my day
- What gives me a buzz at the end of the day
- What am I good at
- How much do I want to be challenged/grow
- Values you want to engage
- Skills and abilities to be used
- What energises you

Feel it: Act As If

When it comes to bringing your dream to life, we need to feel it before seeing it. It's incredible how quickly our thoughts can materialise something in real life. I've already given a few examples throughout this book and often have to stop and acknowledge when it's happening. It is so important to actually validate when you notice the laws working for you. Just today, I had that realisation. It's January, and billings can often be unpredictable at the start of the year. About three weeks ago, I realised I wouldn't achieve much if I didn't put an order out there for what I wanted to achieve financially for the month. So I wrote down a figure that I wanted to show up in my business account by the end of the month, and on the last day of the month, an extra $6,000 turned up from an unpredictable source that helped me achieve my goal.

I'm applying a similar principle while writing this book. As I mentioned, I started writing this book when I started my business four years ago. I finally landed on the title that ignited my inspiration three months ago but still didn't take much action at first. I realised I needed to, so I set a deadline to launch this book on the 12th of April 2022. I pictured the launch day and how proud I'll be to birth my book. Since then, I've reviewed and re-written the chapters in line with the new title, engaged an editor, and have even declared on LinkedIn that the 12th of April will be the launch date, with two chapters still to write. I've even embedded the commitment further by announcing pre-launch sales! It was scary but fabulous. Many people have shown their support and congratulated me. It feels like I'm already a published author. I noticed on LinkedIn that it had even now included Author in my title. I now know that it will happen, and that's inspiring me to keep working on my book each day.

You've probably heard the old saying "fake it til you make it", but that's not what I'm talking about here. That expression has a feeling of deceit about it, of inauthenticity. It is a different feeling when you actually picture your future self already having achieved what you want to achieve.

So I want you to think of how you will feel in your new career, when you're finally aligned with your career purpose. Write down the key characteristics you will display and how you will be, and then do and be those things now. Act as if you've already achieved it, so you act like the person you need to become in that role, and then trust that it will happen.

This brings us to our next chapter. How do you trust it will happen?

Notes:

Notes:

CHAPTER 7

SURRENDER:
Trust & Gratitude

Whatever's truly
meant for you
Won't miss you

[MATT KAHN]

Trust

In Chapter 1, I gave the example of when I was six months into my business and things weren't going according to plan. I was on my morning beach walk, asking myself why everything wasn't falling into place when that trusty whisper entered my head and said "We wouldn't have put you on this path to fail." I took this as a sign to trust. Trust that I was on the right path. Trust that the Universe had my back. Trust that it would all work out.

And so, I trusted, although the path to trusting wasn't quite that simple. Obviously when you're in your own business and supporting yourself and your family, there is a fine line between simply trusting and taking action in order to make things happen. At this point, I want to reiterate Matt Kahn's saying that has helped me trust on many occassions: "whatever is truly meant for you won't miss you". If that's the case, you may say, why bother taking all this action? Whatever will be will be, right?

No! As A Course In Miracles (ACIM) puts it beautifully: "accepting grace does not mean that you simply lie in bed and wait for cheques to float through your window. You were not born to be a passive observer of life. You were born to dive into the adventure and allow a Higher Power to operate through you, as well as for you."

What I've learned is that it is still essential to take action, but without expectation of outcome.

When I was coaching a high volume of job seekers over two years, I observed that when people took their foot off the peddle and backed off on their job search activities, ie stopped applying for other jobs because they were at the second interview stage for one, nothing would happen. Sounds obvious I know but here's the important part. If they kept the momentum going, I observed opportunities start to come their way out of the blue, just not necessarily in the areas they'd been directing their action. I noticed a similar pattern undertaking business development throughout my career. I'd be out and about talking to companies, but then an opportunity would come through from a different company altogether, or from a referral or word of mouth. So as I mentioned, the key is to take action without any expectation, but knowing that it's an essential step in the equation and trust that 'cause and effect' will deliver. It shows that when you are taking action in line with your purpose, the Universe has your back! It might not always look how you planned, or be delivered in your timeframe, but keep the faith that it will happen. Things happen for your highest good and sometimes that means we're not ready yet, or there's something else we need to learn first.

I'm still learning to master the art of surrendering in a few areas of life, although I have come a long way. In my early days working in the recruitment industry, we were trained to pick up the phone and ask a client why we missed out to a competitor, and keep calling until we got them. Now, I place a call to a prospective client and have the attitude that if we're meant to work together, we will. There is no need to control things. In fact, I've often found whenever I've tried to force an outcome, it may work initially, but then it comes undone further down the track. As they say, struggle to get, struggle to keep. We need to consider what energy we're putting into what we're trying to manifest.

This approach creates a far more peaceful way to live life. Remember the Wu Wei way, which encourages us to go with the flow of life, and not fight against it. Whenever I feel like I'm trying to 'get' something to happen, I remind myself to let go. If it's meant for me, it will be. And so it is the same with anything in life, a job, a relationship, a client, an opportunity. Whatever is meant for us will find us.

Gratitude

So where does gratitude fit into our search to get on our path, and pursue our career purpose? As touched on in Chapter 6, it is very difficult to attract something good into our life when we're operating from a place of feeling negative, and operating at a low vibration.

We have a choice to choose our thoughts, so why is it we choose to spend so much time looking at our weaknesses, our shortcomings, and continuously talk about what's not working in our life, and completely overlook what we do have and feel the gratitude? This is one of my current life lessons I'm still in the process of learning, and although it's showing up in an area outside of my career at the moment, I know that life can throw you a challenge to help you build some muscle in one area of your life, so that you can then apply it in other areas. So although this lesson is more personal, I know if something is blocking my gratitude in one area, it's effecting other areas of my life as well. When I stop to think about how it's impacting my career, my business, I know I've come a long way, but it's easy to focus on the distance between where I am now and where I want to be, and not take the time to be grateful for how far I've actually come. And from what I see coaching people, this is a common thought process, and I'm often stopping people to help them acknowledge their growth.

To give you some insight, the area I'm currently being challenged in currently is in relation to my weight gain from four years ago that I haven't been able to shift. I've judged myself so harshly because of it, almost considering myself a lesser person because I can't get control of it. This pattern isn't unusual as in society we end to judge people's success based on a whole lot of superficial criteria. But a shift started to happen not long ago when I reminded myself of the person I am, what I'm here to do, that I've got a good heart, and all I have achieved in my life, and it started to put things in perspective. This is quite a breakthrough for me, and I'm sure many women can relate, because we've been conditioned from a very young age that we're judged on the type of person we are, based on our looks. In ACIM, it talks about the picture and the frame, and how people can be distracted by the frame without really appreciating the picture (the frame being our bodies and the picture, what's inside of us). How can I expect others to appreciate me for me, and not judge me on how I look, if I don't appreciate me and all that I am? This lesson is still a work in progress, and I continue to dig for the gold in this challenge. Stay tuned!

How many times have you felt grateful that you have a body that functions and keeps you alive? Or felt thankful for how amazing your body is, no matter what challenges have come your way? It is common to go about our day not feeling grateful until we're reminded of how lucky we are by a near miss accident or reading the news. How amazing to actually stop and appreciate what you have now, while you have it.

I can remember when my mum passed away, I had so many regrets that I hadn't been more grateful that I'd had her in my life. So don't wait too long to be grateful for the people, and things you have, in your life now.

When we are in a state of gratitude, we are operating at a very high frequency, which as discussed in Chapter 6, then enables us to attract other people, events or things at that frequency. Unless we make time to do this, and shift our mindset, it often doesn't happen. So as part of my morning routine to get me into that higher state, I write down 10 things I'm grateful for. This is what I wrote out this morning and is quite typical of what I usually focus on:

1. My body and all it does for me and enables me to do
2. My health for keeping me independent and functioning
3. My brain for its knowledge, wisdom and what it creates
4. My children for bringing love into my life
5. My home for keeping me safe and giving me shelter and a sense of belonging
6. My business for allowing me to do what I love
7. My clients for allowing me to contribute to them

8. Lenny (our rabbit) for bringing joy into my life
9. My friends for their support and learnings
10. Having money in my bank account to support me.

The purpose of gratitude is to get us in a feelgood state, so don't dwell on those less fortunate to try and make yourself feel grateful for what you do have. You need to approach gratitude with a sense of joy and happiness and really feel it throughout your body.

When you're in a career you're not enjoying it can be challenging to be grateful. When I've been in that position in the past, I've been grateful that the situation has shown me what I don't want and becoming clearer on what I do want. Or I've been grateful that I have a job that is helping me pay the bills, or I remind myself that every day I am moving closer to being on my path. So whenever possible, find a way to shift your thoughts to what you are grateful for.

When you started reading this book, you sensed something was missing in your career. You wanted more meaning and purpose, but as we often do, we rely on others for the answers, to the point where we become blind to our own vision. How can anyone know what's right for you, more than you? You might have had that inner knowing, but for whatever reason, didn't trust your intuition. Just know that when we hear or read something that jumps out at us, it's often because it aligns with something that is true for us. So what have you discovered within this book that has spoken to you?

This book aims to equip you with the knowledge and processes to help you tune in to yourself, and find the answers you are seeking about your path and career purpose. No one will know what rings true for you better than you.

We've covered a lot of ground in this book, and you may be wondering where you need to start. I've created a summary of the steps I've outlined in this book to help you achieve your Career Awakening. However, I want you to tune into your intuition, take a look at the checklist below and see what speaks to you about where you need to start.

Over to you now to forge your path on your path.

Clarity:

Joining The Dots	Review your significant life events, and influences Find out what they were meant to teach you. (Ch 2)
Identify Your Values	Find your values to discover what is intrinsically important to you and help you align your career with your priorities in life. (Ch 4)
Finding Your Career Sweet Spot	Use the Ikigai exercise to ask yourself 4 questions to identify your reason for being. (Ch 4)

 ## Clear:

Identify & Reprogram Beliefs	Look for the patterns so you can identify your blind spots to clear the way for a new future. (Ch 3)
Making Space In Your Life	Peel away the busyness and create a space for something new to show up. (Ch 4)

Create:

	Visualisation	Create a picture of your new future and allow it to become your reality. (Ch 3)
	Exploration Phase	Allow yourself time to explore. Speak to people and get further suggestions and input. (Ch 5)
	Create Your Dream Job Description	Write down what you want. Visualise it. Tell people in your network. (Ch 6)

I hope you now have a strong sense of why you are here and how your life has shaped you, and that you are on the path to becoming the person you want to be. After completing this work, you will know how to read the signs your life shows you and understand that your journey is as much about getting to know you as it is getting to know your path. Appreciating the bumps in the road for what they are, seeing how the Universe has your back and enjoying the ride a little more knowing you're not alone on this journey.

My dream for you is to look at your life and the people, opportunities and challenges that come your way, and see how they serve you and give you clues about your career purpose and path.

Happy journey.

Notes:

Notes:

Career Purpose Courses Available from Creating Healthy Careers at www.creatinghealthycareers.com

Career Clarity
Learn how to tune into your own career guidance system to identify your true career path. This online program will help you find your Career Sweet Spot and align you passion with your profession to have more meaning and purpose in your career.

Purpose Package
This program covers everything in the Career Clarity program, but also gives you access to your own personal Career Coach, me! I'll be by your side to help you discover achieve your desired outcome.

It All Starts With Clarity
This online course will give you a clear vision of your dream job that will enable you to feel valued and will set you up to achieve optimal success and wellbeing in your career. You'll rediscover and reconnect with who you are and what you love, and identify your value proposition and how to align this with your dream job.

Your Career DNA
In this online course, you will learn how to find the clues that life has been showing you about your career all along. You'll identify what's important to you in finding the fulfillment you're looking for, and feel a sense of pride that you're finally following your path. I'll show you how to dig for the clues in your past and bring it together to identify your Career Sweet Spot.

Breaking Past Patterns
This course will help you to identify what's been holding you back in your career. You'll finally see your blind spots and they'll no longer be a barrier to your success. You'll discover what's been getting in the way, how to reprogram those beliefs and programs and then create a new future.

Make It Happen
Now you have the clarity about your path, how do you make it happen? Learn the tips from a career recruiter that will have your resume and cover letter stand out from the competition, find the hidden jobs, and have you performing at your best at interview.

Elevate Career Coaching Program
This 1:1 program allows you to take a step out of your career and see what's truly going on, and then step back in, empowered and successful. You will take a deep dive into: understanding your career DNA by looking at your values and value proposition, clear any career blocks, do a career health check and look at some wellbeing strategies to power your career, and create your new reality.

Career Breakthrough Program
This program will have you working 1:1 with me to help you breakthrough what's really holding you back from taking off and achieving the next level of success in your career. It's a customisable approach to elevating your career and helping you achieve success in a sustainable way. This program focuses on 6 key pillars to help you remove barriers, reassess what's truly important to you and reignite your career.

Notes:

Notes:

www.ingramcontent.com/pod-product-compliance
Lightning Source LLC
Chambersburg PA
CBHW070307010526
44107CB00056B/2518